Praise for
More Ghost Chronicles

"With so much content out there from purported paranormal experts, it is difficult to know whom to turn to for honest yet compelling accounts. Look no further than this book! Maureen Wood and Ron Kolek have been there and done that when it comes to the supernatural. Cozy up with a warm blanket, turn the lights down, and enter their world of the weird in *More Ghost Chronicles*. I assure you a frightful time but in a very good way."

—JIM HAROLD, host of *The Paranormal Podcast* and *Campfire*

"Delightfully wicked in all the right ways, Ron and Maureen do not disappoint with their ghostly tales of lighthouses, drunken sailors, old mills, and the mysterious Puckwudgie of legend and lore. You'll devour their wonderful stories from cover to cover."

—VARLA VENTURA, author of *Varla Ventura's Paranormal Parlor*

"*More Ghost Chronicles* is like traveling with your best friends across a bridge between the seen and the unseen worlds. Maureen and Ron share their vantage point of this connecting, energetic matrix so we all can learn how these two worlds affect each other and how they affect us. It is a journey both entertaining and educational with plenty of what-the-heck and that-makes-sense moments."

—JUANITA VIOLINI, author of *Almanac of the Infamous, the Incredible, and the Ignored*

"New England, known for its haunting stories of ghosts and terror in the night, now brings you bone-chilling tales of an actual investigator and a psychic who take readers deep into the heart and soul of darkness. Each story in *More Ghost Chronicles* is more compelling than the last, taking you to your innermost core, filled with the fear of what the unknown can truly do! Images of what it's like to take on the spirits—as authors Kolek and Wood try to unravel the mysteries of what lies behind the veil—will have you gripping your blankets with the lights on."

—KRISTIN LEE, owner of the Bellaire House and
author of *1699 Belmont Street: A Portal to Hell*

"Ron Kolek and Maureen Wood took me to a place I swore I'd never go. After investigating the ghosts of Gettysburg for several decades, I've collected and experienced some of the most bizarre things one can imagine: phantom gunfire; an elevator opening onto a Civil War hospital scene; the ghostly, blue face of a little boy peering into a window three floors up; human blood on the floor of a historic hospital from the Battle of Gettysburg that disappeared completely. So you might say I've become jaded to the fright inherent in the paranormal. But the one thing I swore I never wanted to witness was the channeling of a tormented spirit by a trance medium. Well, thanks to Ron and Maureen's visit to Gettysburg recounted in *More Ghost Chronicles*—this wonderful, impossible-to-put-down book—I watched horrified as Maureen channeled the ghost of a wounded soldier about to go under the scalpel at the Daniel Lady Farm hospital. It scared the living bejeebers out of me. This and other tales of their adventures at sites steeped in the supernatural will do the same for you."

—MARK NESBITT, author of the *Ghosts of Gettysburg* series

More
Ghost
Chronicles

**Stories from the realm
of the unknown, the
unexplained, and
the unbelievable**

**Maureen Wood
and Ron Kolek**

Foreword by Jeff Belanger

WEISER BOOKS

This edition first published in 2018 by Weiser Books, an imprint of
Red Wheel/Weiser, LLC

With offices at:
65 Parker Street, Suite 7
Newburyport, MA 01950
www.redwheelweiser.com

ISBN: 978-1-57863-635-8

Library of Congress Cataloging-in-Publication Data

Names: Wood, Maureen, author.
Title: More ghost chronicles : stories from the realm of the unknown, the
   unexplained, and the unbelievable / Maureen Wood and Ron Kolek ;
foreword
   by Jeff Belanger.
Description: Newburyport : Weiser Books, 2018.
Identifiers: LCCN 2018018506 | ISBN 9781578636358 (6 x 9 pbk. : alk.
paper)
Subjects: LCSH: Ghosts. | Haunted places. | Channeling (Spiritualism) |
   Parapsychology.
Classification: LCC BF1461 .W663 2018 | DDC 133.1—dc23
LC record available at https://lccn.loc.gov/2018018506

Cover design by Kathryn Sky-Peck
Cover photo by iStock
Interior by Maureen Forys, Happenstance Type-O-Rama
Typeset in ITC Oldbook, Formata and Old Newspaper Types

Printed in Canada
MAR

10 9 8 7 6 5 4 3 2 1

Dedication

Maureen:

To my late mother: Thank you for always being my rock and for loving me unconditionally. You always were, and still are, my biggest champion. I love you.

To my husband: What can I say . . . you are my love, my life, and my best friend on this crazy ride we call life.

To my daughter, Sabrina; my son, Joshua; and his beautiful wife, Kimberly: When others in this world are not so kind in their acceptance of my abilities, your belief, love, and support in who I am have meant more to me than you could possibly know. I love you all with every fiber of my being. Thank you.

Last, but certainly not least, to Addison, my granddaughter, who at the age of two is already displaying medium/psychic abilities: It is my hope that this book may someday act as a guide to help you understand that what you are experiencing is completely normal. Or should I say paranormal? And if nothing else, Sweetie, know that you are not alone. May the light inside you shine brightly for all to see, and may you never fear the gifts that God has given you. I love you more than words can say. By the way, your new nickname, since I am the fifth-generation psychic and your mom is number six, well, I guess that makes you lucky number seven!

Ron:

I would like to dedicate this book to Thermal Dan. Daniel E. Parsons was the deputy fire chief for the town of Hamilton for over twenty years, the squadron commander of the Beverly Civil Air Patrol, and a trusted member of the New England Ghost Project. He introduced our team to thermal imaging and gave us the rare opportunity to investigate two vintage B17s. He loved his son, Kent, often missing investigations to watch him compete in swim meets on the college level. Dan, we miss you, and I am sure our paths will cross again someday.

Lastly, I want to thank, St. Jan, my wife, and also my loving mother, both of whom put up with me all these years, never wavering in their love for me.

Contents

Foreword

Why do we do it?

Why do we expend so much of our free time and money to lurk in dark buildings, creepy woods, abandoned places, and locales where oftentimes tragic history has left a permanent scar on the location and our collective psyche?

The reason can be found somewhere deep inside us . . . in the very primal parts of the human experience—those places that understand urges like survival. We believe we'll find answers to the biggest question humankind has ever asked: what happens after we die?

See a ghost or spirit, and suddenly you have some clarity on that inquiry. Who can blame you for wanting to tell others what you've found? So we tell the public through writing and speaking about the fringe on radio programs and at conferences or to anyone who will listen. We get feedback from both skeptic and believer and adjust our own point of view or maybe solidify our beliefs after sharing our experiences with others. We search for ghosts, for things that go bump in the night, and we chase stories, because in doing so we become a part of those tales and lore. . . . It can be addictive.

I've known Ron Kolek and Maureen Wood since 2004. My first book had just been published, and I was searching for places to promote it. When you study and write about the paranormal, finding venues to discuss your work is a challenge. Fortunately,

2004 was back when the Internet was still blossoming and connecting people with similar interests like never before. The paranormal discussion was beginning on a grand scale through multiple media outlets—we were all there to be a part of it. For the first time in human history, millions were learning they're not alone in their supernatural experiences.

We've been talking about it ever since.

In those early days, I would tag along with Ron and Maureen on investigations, or we'd see each other at conferences and events, and I got to see them in action. Yes, they are like an old married couple, but I've learned that connection yields results. Between Maureen's intuition and Ron's objectivity and gadgets, they connect with something that's just beyond the grasp for most of us.

I've watched them learn to anticipate the other's next move, and to bicker about what it could or couldn't be that's sitting there just beyond the veil. But disagreeing and respectful arguing are good things. It's important to debate. It's good not to agree all of the time and important to listen to other perspectives on this subject.

Here's the thing about the ghost experience: you can't put it in a jar and hold it up to a microscope. But what you're holding in your hands right now is the next best thing. These are some of the case files of two investigators who have a passion for experiencing and chronicling the unexplained. Both individuals are well seasoned and highly knowledgeable.

These pages will take you through the haunts, detail why Ron and Maureen were called in to investigate, and show you what they experienced and discovered. Ron's data and observations, plus Maureen's psychic impressions, make for a haunting adventure. If you're ready to investigate for yourself, you can use this as a guide for one way to do it. Or, if you prefer to keep your ghosts and elementals at arm's length, you can sit back and watch Ron and Maureen put themselves into potential peril, while you're safely on the other side of the book.

Mortality is something we all must face. The first promise we're given as infants is that we're going to die one day. What comes next? Will we somehow survive the passing of our physical bodies? And if so, who would *you* haunt? One day we all might end up as a page in a paranormal investigator's ghost files.

—JEFF BELANGER, author of *The World's Most Haunted Places* and host of *New England Legends*

Acknowledgments

Maureen:

Dear reader, thank you for taking this journey through the Ghost Chronicles—to walk hand in hand and experience the surreal paranormal investigations through each of our perspectives. You may not be aware, but prior to writing each episode, and in an attempt to provide you with as much factual accuracy as possible, Ron and I revisited each piece of audio and video that had been captured during the investigations, along with the transcripts—so much so that our efforts got to the point of being painful. Why? Well, for those of you who don't know me, I am not what you would call photogenic. I guess you could call it a phobia of sorts, as I find myself very uncomfortable while facing a camera lens. I dislike viewing myself in photos and videos—to the point that it becomes extremely painful to watch. Especially during a channeling session. Nevertheless, to provide our readers with anything less than our best effort would be unacceptable. So, sit back and buckle yourself in, because you're in for a wild ride.

Ron:

As I grow older, I am getting closer to my own finality. Yet I do not fear death. Nor do I embrace it but rather have learned more to understand it. My thirst for knowledge has led me on this journey, and I will continue to learn and question until the very end. Understanding is what drives me and the New

England Ghost Project. As you read this book and our first one, *The Ghost Chronicles*, you will experience what it is like for me to be on this quest and how my personal beliefs have changed along the way. So, grab your coffee, tea, or something stronger and share the ride.

Introduction

Ron Kolek, founder of the New England Ghost Project, was a skeptic and scientist on a quest to validate the paranormal. Maureen Wood, on the other hand, had talked to the dead all of her life. She knew ghosts existed. What brought these two together was the desire to help both the living and the dead. Ron with his electromagnetic field (EMF) meter and Maureen with her pendulum have learned to walk the fine line that separates the realms of the living and the dead. Whether it's dealing with an ancient evil, consoling the ghost of a mournful bride, solving the mysteries of a windswept lighthouse, or connecting with the lost souls of America's bloodiest battlefields, it's all in a day's (or night's!) work for the New England Ghost Project.

In *More Ghost Chronicles*, the journey continues. In the desolate forest of the Bridgewater Triangle, the team repels multiple attacks from the foul presence of a primeval elemental. The resulting video was so astonishing that it went viral, ending up in a feature film and on the television series *Monsters and Mysteries in America*.

Meanwhile, on the foggy coast of Maine, the ghost bride of Cape Elizabeth summons Maureen to share in her grief, recounting the tale of her premature demise in hopes of finding peace.

While filming an Emmy-winning Halloween special for *American Builder*, the team solves the mystery of an urban legend when they encounter the angry spirit of a lighthouse. The frightening confrontation changes the perceptions of Jimmy, the show's skeptical host.

During a visit to Gettysburg, the chilling voices of departed soldiers reach out from beyond the grave to make their presence known. An onslaught of ghostly encounters ensues: the spirit of an amputee at a field hospital, a priest taking up residence in a modern hotel, and even sentries still on guard on the battlefields of Gettysburg.

These are but some of the untold tales that continue to color their perceptions of life, death, and the paranormal. Whether it's helping the living or dealing with the dead, *More Ghost Chronicles* provides a unique perspective into the lives of people touched by the paranormal. Ron, with his down-to-earth scientific approach, and Maureen, with her psychic insight, take you on yet another journey into the realm of the unknown, the unexplained, and the unbelievable. Readers become virtual members of their team as they unravel the mysteries of each and every case. They experience the laughter, tears, and fears that are sometimes associated with investigating the paranormal. You'll learn why Maureen is known as the Queen of Pain and why Ron is, well, he's just . . . a pain.

More
Ghost
Chronicles

The Reverend's Secret

Case File: 1904323 The Reverend's Secret

Location: A small New Hampshire town

History: A white historic farmhouse with attached barn and apartment, located in the old part of town.

Reported Paranormal Activity: The feeling of being watched. Doors opening and closing of their own accord. Apparitions and visitations accompanied by strange inexplicable noises.

Clients: Homeowners: Mary; her husband, Ben; sons William, Frank, and Al; along with their tenant, a medium named Dawn.

Investigators: Ron (lead investigator), Maureen (trance medium), Ron Jr. (investigator/photographer), Jim (photographer), Karen Mossey (EVP specialist), St. Jan (Ron's wife).

Press: N/A.

Purpose of Investigation: To validate the experiences of the homeowner and her family.

It was 5:59 p.m. "Well, we're out of time, so remember to tune in every Friday from five to six for another episode of *Ghost Chronicles* here on WCCM." Maureen and I spoke in unison, "Good night and God bless."

Over the heartbeats of the closing, Lou said, "Mics are off. You two are good to go."

With that I removed my headset, dropped it on the desk, and jumped to my feet, sending the office chair rolling against the wall. Maureen and I scrambled down the corridor, out the station's door, and into her Audi A6. *I guess we're driving in style tonight.*

Fighting the typical Friday night traffic jam heading north on 93, we arrived at our destination in the old part of Salem, New Hampshire.

No sooner had we arrived than I heard the horn blow and glanced in the rearview mirror to see Jim's van pull in behind us. Like the exiting of a clown mobile, the rest of the crew piled out of his Aerostar.

"I thought I'd beat you guys here." Jim chuckled.

"Seriously? With that Aerostar? Slim chance," Maureen retorted.

Without even enough time to collect ourselves, we were greeted by a group of enthusiastic people in the driveway.

As I looked past the mob that had assembled, I couldn't help but notice the historic nature of this circa-1825 house and attached barn. In fact, it was just as Mary, the homeowner, had described in our previous conversation.

"Hi, Ron," Mary said in a greeting. "I recognize you from *Channel 5 Chronicles.*"

"I'm better looking in person, you know," I said, as I glanced at Maureen, who was rolling her eyes as usual.

Mary gestured to the group that was now gathering closer. "This is my husband, Ben, my sons William, Frank, and Al." She looked at Maureen and then reached out to touch the arm of the woman standing next to her. "And this is Dawn. She rents an apartment here. She's a medium, too, you know."

"Nice to meet you," I said, but what I thought was, *Whatever. Everyone's a medium these days.*

"You want to come this way," Mary said as she motioned us to follow.

One by one we walked through the old barn door and up a set of creaky wooden steps and into the kitchen. We stood elbow to elbow around the kitchen island, packed in like sardines. Although it was distracting, we had to deal with it, nevertheless. I looked at Maureen, and I didn't have to be psychic to know she was thinking the same thing I was: *This is way too many people to conduct a proper investigation.*

Looking at Ron, I read his thoughts. This was way too many people to conduct a proper investigation. Above the clamor of voices, the all-too-familiar feeling began to arise. My heart began to beat wildly in my chest. A spirit had arrived. Typically, I would walk throughout the room to scan the energy. To my frustration, the large crowd and lack of space prevented this. Feeling like I was being beckoned, I weaved through the crowd to what appeared to be a walled-up chimney. My heart beat even faster. The energy was extremely strong here. I reached out and placed my palm on the painted brick. Like a hand on a hot stove, I jerked it back as a sharp pain shot through me. "Freakin' A!" I yelped as I clutched my head.

"What's wrong?" Ron asked, maneuvering closer.

"I don't know. There's something weird in there."

"Weird how?"

Apparently eavesdropping on our conversation, Dawn spoke up, "There's nothing bad here. I know; I'm a medium."

I looked at her and smiled through gritted teeth. Maybe that's what you feel, but the world's not all rainbows and unicorns, I thought to myself. I reached out my hand to touch the brick once again. This time nothing.

"Do you want to communicate here?" Ron asked.

I shook my head no. Whatever had been here a moment ago was now gone.

Ron Jr. interrupted. "Dad, you can forget about recording an interview. You're not going to believe this. The camcorder batteries are dead."

"You're kidding me. I just charged them."

"Evidently you didn't bless them," I said. By the oh-shit look that crossed Ron's face, I guess I was right.

Ron turned toward Mary who was wrapped up in a conversation with Ron Jr. "Okay, where's this door that keeps opening by itself. You know, the one you told me about the other day."

"It's upstairs. Follow me," she said, as she motioned to an adjacent room.

We followed her, climbed the stairs to the second-floor hallway. Halfway down the corridor, I could feel the light, playful energy of a child. Taking advantage of the moment, I stopped mid-step, closed my eyes, and concentrated. The energetic signature was unmistakable. I knew it was a little girl. "Ron, hold up."

He stopped in his tracks and turned back at me. "What d'ya get?"

I reached out, gliding my hand back and forth in the corridor's atmosphere. "It's a little girl. I can feel her run past me, over and over. Like she's playing with us."

Ron, with a tight grip on the EMF he was holding, began to wave it up and down. "I got nothing."

EMF (ELECTROMAGNETIC FIELD) METER

A handheld electronic device used to measure electromagnetic radiation in milligauss. This instrument is widely used by paranormal investigators to identify normal sources of EMF, such as fluorescent lights and electrical wiring, as well as unexplained sources of EMF associated with paranormal activity.

"I know she's here." The moment I said it, I heard an ethereal whisper in my ear: My name is Sarah. "Her name is Sarah."

"How do you know that?"

"She just told me," I said fighting back tears. My heart suddenly heavy, filled with grief, I said, "Oh, my God. She died in a fire."

Mary, now listening, interjected. "There was no fire here that we know of."

I shrugged in response. "I can only tell you what she told me." Even though in my heart I knew it was true.

I reached out with my mind, returning my attention back to Sarah once again. But she was gone. "Sarah apparently has nothing else to say. She's left." I turned to Ron. "I think we can move on now."

Taking Maureen's advice, we continued down the hallway to the master bedroom. I rounded the corner and found myself staring at a large poster on the closet door. "Hey, look at this," I said, pointing to the poster that was floating to and fro off the door. "Ron Jr., take a picture."

Ron Jr. raised his camera and snapped the button to take a shot. Nothing. He tried again, to no avail.

Not wanting to lose the moment, I reached for my own camera and raised it to my eye. But before I had a chance to take a picture, the camera flew out of my hand and crashed to the wide-plank floor. "What the hell?! It felt like someone just whacked it out of my hand," I said as I picked up the now-broken camera and dropped it atop the dresser. I cautiously approached the still-moving poster. I opened the case clipped to my belt and retrieved the anemometer, taking various measurements around the poster.

> ## ANEMOMETER
>
> A handheld device used for measuring wind speed. The term *anemometer* is derived from the Greek word *Anemos,* which translates as "wind." The first recorded description of an anemometer was given by Leon Battista Alberti in 1450. Some meters also record temperature.

I could detect no draft. But still the poster moved. Glancing at the gauge on the anemometer, I did notice a drop in temperature. I turned around and spied Maureen standing by the rocking chair, which appeared to be moving of its own accord. "Maureen, do you feel anything?"

Maureen didn't respond right away. Placing her hand to her temple, she said, "Yes. In fact, I think there are two spirits here. A woman and a man."

"Who are you connected with?"

"The woman. I think it's the little girl's mother." Rubbing her temple, she grimaced and shook her head as though she was struggling with something. "She keeps trying to relay a message, but . . . the other spirit—the man—is trying to stop her from speaking."

She removed her hand from her forehead, stood erect, and took a deep breath. "His thoughts are coming through clearer now." She groaned in disgust. "I can feel his loathing for this woman and her child."

As if the words were torn from her body, she screeched, "Whore!"

A sudden look of horror crossed Maureen's face. "Oh, my God. Sarah is his daughter. That's disgusting. He's a reverend."

"He was a reverend?" I asked.

Mary spoke up, "A reverend did live here."

Maureen bent over in pain, then stumbled back. "I can feel his rage. He's angry because his secret's been revealed." Hands on her thighs, Maureen slowly straightened herself. Through raspy breath, she said, "He's gone."

Puzzled, Mary looked to Dawn. "What do *you* think?"

Dawn stood there, jaw clenched, remaining silent.

Mary huffed and spoke up again. "Like I said, a reverend did live here. But there's no record of a Sarah or any other child by him."

As in the hallway, Maureen shrugged. Her voice curt, "Right or wrong, all I can say is what comes to me."

Not wanting to get into a pissing match between two mediums and trying to diffuse the situation, I turned to Karen, who had been recording the whole time. "Karen, did you get anything?"

EVP (ELECTRONIC VOICE PHENOMENON)

When a spirit manifests its voice on an electronic device such as a digital recorder by manipulating the white noise. EVPs are not heard by the naked ear but can be heard later on playback. The most popular device for capturing EVPs is Panasonic's DR60.

"Let me check." She pressed the replay button of her digital recorder and raised it to her ear. The room grew silent. Through the small speakers of the recorder we could hear what sounded like a sermon being recited.

"Wow, did you hear that?" Karen said as she rewound the recorder and hit play again.

Mary and Dawn leaned closer, listening more intently.

Once again, a man's voice echoed through the speaker. "We are all gathered here . . ."

Mary was giddy with excitement. "Dawn, did you hear that? Wow, that was amazing, Karen."

Both Mary and Dawn stood in front of Maureen and me, enthusiastically chatting with Karen as if she were a long-lost friend.

"That was cool, but we still have to check out the rest of the house. Let's move on," I said.

A short time later, Maureen and I were back in the Audi driving home. Because of the equipment issues and drained batteries, I had to listen to her rant and rave all the way home about not blessing the equipment.

"I got it," I spat. "By the way, I don't think they were too happy about your assessment of the reverend."

"Oh, well. And why have us come and investigate if they were so sure of what was going on there? Whatever."

Three months later I received a phone call from Mary, who conveyed that after Dawn moved out, they had received a strange message on their answering machine. Mary asked me to call her back and listen. I dialed the number, and as the answering machine message played, I couldn't believe my ears. Immediately after, I called Maureen at work. "Do you remember that investigation we did in Salem, with the reverend and the little girl, Sarah?"

"Yeah."

"Do you remember how they didn't believe you and told us there was no record of any Sarah ever having lived there?"

An exasperated sigh came through the phone. "How could I forget?"

"Well, I just got a call from Mary."

"And?"

"Well, just call this number and listen to the answering machine. Then call me back."

———————

Without hesitation, I dialed the number Ron had given me and listened. The eerie whispers of a little girl's voice could be heard beneath the outgoing welcome message, "Across the road . . . follow the wall . . . down by the river . . . by the big oak tree . . . you will find me."

As cool as it was, I was confused. Not sure what to make of it, I called Ron back. "Hi, Ron. I heard the message. What the hell does it mean?"

Ron chuckled. "You're gonna love this. If you follow the instructions, it leads you to a small grave. There, etched in the cold stone is the name Sarah."

I smiled to myself. "It appears the reverend's secret has been revealed."

OUR THOUGHTS

MAUREEN:

As a medium, I know it takes a leap of faith to voice the information that is being received. Even if the information is not in line with what is expected—or perceived to be accurate at the time. Why a spirit chooses to be heard and the messages they give are anybody's guess.

There are no guarantees for anything in life. Or death. We are dealing with the unknown. So, in this case, especially with everything that transpired, I am extremely grateful to Sarah for validating her existence to the homeowner. She was one little girl who demanded to be heard. Maybe now she can find the peace she so rightfully deserves.

RON:

At the end of the night, we had little physical evidence. Karen captured one EVP of note, we witnessed a poster that appeared to move by itself without any obvious environmental influence, and my camera was mysteriously knocked out of my hand. Maureen's impressions were enlightening as always but seemed to conflict with the other psychic who was there. However, the strange message discovered under the welcoming message on the homeowners' answering machine that led them to the little girl's grave brought me great satisfaction in that it validated what Maureen had told us.

Tricks at Rick's

Case File: 1904052 Rick's Cafe

Location: Kingston, New Hampshire

History: Built during the Revolutionary War, this home-turned-restaurant is located in Kingston, one of New Hampshire's most historic towns.

Reported Paranormal Activity: Eerie mists, slithering shadows, objects moving by themselves.

Clients: Rick Korn (restaurant owner).

Investigators: Ron (lead investigator), Maureen (trance medium), Ron Jr. (investigator), Karen (EVP specialist), Jim (photographer), St. Jan (Ron's wife).

Press: Eric Baxter and his photographer, Bruce (*The Salem Observer*); Margo Lesage (*Lawrence Eagle-Tribune*).

Purpose of Investigation: Providing the press with the opportunity to experience a paranormal investigation, while attempting to discover the reasons behind the odd occurrences at the restaurant.

I had arranged to do an investigation at a restaurant in Derry, New Hampshire, when it was cancelled at the last minute. A cancellation would normally not be a problem, except that I had invited Margo Lesage from the *Lawrence Eagle-Tribune* and

Eric Baxter from the *Salem Observer* to come along. I needed to
find another place quick, so I called Rick Korn at Rick's Cafe in
Kingston. Rick jumped at the chance to investigate his restaurant, and the stage was set for the evening encounter. But what
would we encounter?

Later that night, after a short trip, we arrived at what appeared
to be an older home that had been converted into a restaurant.
We piled out of the van and entered through an old heavy-duty
hardwood door. As I surveyed the room, I noticed Eric and his
photographer, Bruce, had already arrived and were speaking
with what appeared to be some of the staff.

As the door slammed behind us, Eric looked over his shoulder. "Hey, Ron. You finally made it. Glad you're here. I was getting worried."

The kitchen door swung open behind Eric, and I saw the
small frame of a woman walk through. I knew, unmistakably,
that it was Margo.

Ron Jr. plopped the equipment down on one of the dining room
tables by the window and began setting up base camp. A second
later, I heard him calling me, "Dad, can you give me a hand."

———·—·———

As I stepped through the entryway past Ron and Ron Jr., I imme-
diately felt the onslaught of energy that began gnawing at me. I
reached into my fleece jacket to pull out my rosary beads and cringed.

ROSARY BEADS

A Roman Catholic ritual object comprising a string or necklace of beads, divided
into five sets of ten beads that are used to count off a series of prayers. The
word *rosary* means "crown of roses."

They weren't there. I frantically searched my other pockets to no avail. "Crapstick," I grumbled. I don't know what I was thinking. How could I forget something that's such a staple in my protection during an investigation? Nervously, I stepped over to Ron. "You're not going to believe this, but I forgot my rosary beads."

"Oh, there's a big surprise. You're always forgetting everything. Sometimes I feel like I'm your purse." He hesitated, then dug into the pocket of his jeans. "Here, take these," he said, as he plopped the delicate beads into my open palm. "Be careful with these—they were my father's."

Once the beads were in my hand, I looked them over and noticed the details—muted browns and blacks, slightly aged, but beautiful just the same. I could almost feel the memories vibrating along their surface. Realizing their sentiment, I was a bit nervous and determined to take extra good care of them. I held them gently between my fingers, draped over my palms, while Bruce, the photographer, stood close by. Now that the equipment had been set up, Ron began to interview the waitstaff. Ron Jr. videotaped the interviews while I stood off to the side.

Through all the commotion, I began to feel a surge of energy swirling around me. The sudden pressure in my forehead could only mean one thing: whatever had been haunting Rick's had joined me now and was listening to every word spoken. I turned my head slowly and scanned the room, looking for someone who may be feeling what I was feeling. I didn't have to look too far for a sign.

Ron Jr. fiddled with the camera. "Hold on, Dad. Looks like this freakin' battery is dead."

Suddenly, I felt a rush of energy brushing up against me. I extended the rosaries out in front of me, between both hands. As if struck by some unseen force, the rosary broke in two. Just great! The rosary beads I'd held so gently in my hands were now split in two.

"Did I see right?" the photographer asked with a quiver in his voice.

"Yes," I said, still trying to absorb what had just happened.

He aimed his camera at the beads I held in my hand and began clicking away.

Whammo!

Whatever was playing games with me split the rosary once again. I cringed as I heard the sound of the beads bouncing off the wooden floor.

"Oh, my God! Did you see that?" the photographer exclaimed.

Ignoring his question, I nervously bent over and gathered up the scattered beads from the floor and placed them all in the palm of my hand. Now what? My feet suddenly feeling like lead, I reluctantly headed toward Ron, feeling like a person being sent to the gallows. Nervously, I spoke up, "Hey, Ron, did you give me a broken rosary to hold?"

———————

I looked at Maureen, giving her one of my "Yeah, right!" stares, and replied, "Sure, I always carry broken rosaries with me." With that she dropped the fragments on the table. Shocked, I asked her what had happened. She went on to explain the weird circumstances of their demise as she attempted to reassemble them. Feeling uneasy about her efforts, I said, "They're linked in groups of ten, you know."

Raising her eyebrows, she replied sarcastically, "Really?! I didn't know that."

With that, I scooped them up from the table and stuffed them in my pocket.

"Okay, Dad, I put a new battery in the camera. We can pick up where we left off."

Still miffed, I glared at Maureen one last time before turning my attention back to the interviews. Next, a dark-haired woman took a seat on the stool in front of us.

"Hi, what's your name, and how long have you worked here?" I asked.

She spoke up in a demure voice. "My name is Meredith Smith, and I've worked here for the last four years."

"Have you had any paranormal experiences while working here?"

"Have I? Let me tell you, the ghost likes to play tricks with us." She nervously adjusted herself on the wooden stool and continued. "Since I started working here, lights would turn on and off by themselves. Locked doors would open of their own accord. And let me tell you about the basement. I hate going into the basement. One time I heard whistling down there and there was no one around. And perhaps the most unnerving thing was that muddy footprints appeared on the basement floor out of nowhere."

"Oh, wow. Do you have anything else to add?"

"No. But there's another waitress here by the name of Katie. She goes down into the basement to smoke. On several occasions, while smoking, her half-smoked cigarettes will disappear from the ashtray."

Rick spoke up, "I have got a real weird one for you." He hesitated for a minute, as if to gather his thoughts. "I have a sign outside my upstairs office, and one day when I came in, there were chicken bones on the top of the sign. This is really weird because we don't serve chicken on the bone here. They were also covered in spider webs, like they had been there for months. I really can't explain that." He adjusted his stance and continued. "And the chicken bones aren't even the weirdest things I've experienced." He scratched his chin. "We have a big Braun stainless steel coffeemaker in the kitchen. On many occasions, the filter has been seen becoming dislodged from the unit and flies across the room." Barely taking a breath, he added, "If you don't believe me, you can ask any of the staff. They've all seen it."

"Trust me, after doing this for so long, I've heard everything and seen everything. At this point, nothing surprises me." I chuckled.

I took a moment to glance around the room. "If anybody else has anything to add, now's the time to speak up." Silence was my answer. "Okay, let's start the investigation."

I gathered up the team, and we started a sweep of the building with the staff and the reporters in tow. Janet stayed behind and monitored our progress from base camp. We passed through the kitchen and down the stairs into the basement. Before we even reached the bottom of the stairs, my EMF meter came to life. Judging from the look on Maureen's face, I knew that she was sensing whatever or whoever was here.

———

The red glow of Ron's EMF meter illuminated our surroundings, casting strange shadows on the cold damp walls. As we snaked our way through the shelves and boxes arranged in the basement, the energy grew stronger. When we reached the back room, it was overwhelming. It was evident to me that the spirit that had been dogging us was ready to communicate. I pulled out my pendulum, hoping I'd have better results than I did with Ron's rosary beads.

PENDULUM/SPIRITUAL DOWSING

Using a pendulum (a weighted bobber on a string or chain) to communicate with the dead via a series of rotations. The various rotations indicate yes, no, and maybe responses, and they vary from person to person, depending on their own energy.

Within a few moments, a name popped into the forefront of my thoughts. "His name is Irving Nason."

Suddenly, I felt the eyes of the group focused on me. I proceeded to ask questions. "Were you the owner of this establishment?"

In a strong rotation, the pendulum replied, "Yes."

"Did you die here?"

Once again, the pendulum swung counterclockwise, denoting a yes. My concentration was briefly broken when out of the corner of my eye I noticed the light on Karen's recorder, flashing, indicating a response as well.

We continued to ask questions, as the pendulum spun and twirled in response.

Ron's meter beeped wildly while the spirit's strength escalated, feeding off the combined energy of the room. Along with the escalation and its strength came the accompanied pain I often feel. It too had become nearly unbearable.

Ron, aware of my discomfort, reached for the blood pressure cuff he had brought along. I'd been telling Ron since we had been investigating together, when the energy gets so intense, I feel it in my heart, like a sharp pain. It was getting me nervous. I found myself wondering if this would kill me at some point. So, Ron had this bright idea to bring a digital blood pressure cuff to this investigation to monitor my health. I really wasn't sure about this. It suddenly felt as if we were bringing a knife to a gun fight.

Ron held the blood pressure cuff in his hands, "Are you going to give me your arm or what?"

Still a bit tentative, I obliged and added, "I've got a bad feeling about this."

"You always have a bad feeling about everything," Ron chided, as he placed the cuff around my upper arm and proceeded to inflate it.

As Ron continued to squeeze the bulb, the pressure mounted. The digital readout was nothing but wild lines and bars spinning in rapid succession. But it didn't deter him, and he continued to pump away.

"*For crying out loud! Are you trying to kill me?*"

"*What? It worked fine upstairs.*"

"*Stop it!*" *I screamed.* "*Apparently, the spirit's up to his tricks again.*"

"*Oh, you're such a big baby.*"

Thankfully with the last of his words, he released the valve. The blood returning to my arm was heaven. As the feeling returned to my arm, the energy that had been so strong began to quickly dissipate.

"*I think Irving's gone.*" Ron's EMF meter went silent.

"*Okay then. I guess it's time to go upstairs. Irving has spoken. Follow me,*" Ron said.

Ron led the procession out of the cellar and up the old wooden stairs. I stood there for a moment while each member of the team walked passed me, busily chatting among themselves. I reached out to grab the bannister, and as I ascended the stairs, each of my steps on the stairs grew more difficult. It seemed like the more I climbed each step, the heavier my feet became.

I felt horrible.

My breathing was labored. I inhaled deeply in an attempt to catch my breath, to no avail. Suddenly, I became dizzy and felt as if someone or something had reached into my chest and squeezed my heart in their invisible grip.

By the time I reached the top of the stairs, there was no one in sight. I felt as if I needed a breath of fresh air. Once outside, I reached into my back pocket and pulled out Ron's St. Michael's prayer card. Standing beneath the wall sconce by the back door, I began to recite the prayer:

> **St. Michael, the Archangel, defend us in battle.**
> **Be our protection against the malice and snares of the devil.**
> **May God rebuke him, we humbly pray. . . .**

The light went out. Suddenly, I was in complete darkness.

Unable to continue reciting the prayer, I stopped. And just as quickly as it went out, the light came back on. Just as the light came on, the door swung open and Karen stepped through it. "I was looking for you," she said. "Are you all right?"

"I think so. But I was trying to read this prayer, and the light went out for no reason."

"Really?"

"Let's try reading it together." I paused for a moment. "Do you mind?"

In unison we began to read:

> **St. Michael, the Archangel, defend us in battle.**
> **Be our protection against the malice and snares of the devil.**
> **May God rebuke him, we humbly pray. . . .**

Once again, just as before, the light went out. "Are you serious?"

Not wanting to lose the moment, we tried again with the same result. "Karen, go get Ron."

"Good idea!" she said as she darted through the door. It slammed behind her.

Within moments, Karen returned with Ron.

After a brief explanation, the three of us attempted to recite the prayer again:

> **St. Michael, the Archangel, defend us in battle.**
> **Be our protection against the malice and snares of the devil.**
> **May God rebuke him, we humbly pray. . . .**

Before we could recite the next verse, the light went out again. A collective gasp escaped our lips.

"Cool," Ron said. "Let me go get Margo."

The light now on, Ron returned with Margo and the photographer.

For the umpteenth time, I began to recite the prayer again, but this time, I was able to finish the whole prayer as the light remained on. I couldn't help but notice Margo's lackluster stare. This made me wonder if she thought I'd just fallen off the crazy train. What asses spirits can be. Instead of our experiences being verified by Margo, she witnessed nothing.

"It seems this spirit has a penchant for playing tricks." I tucked the prayer card back into my pocket, "Looks like it's going to get the last laugh."

"I think it's time to wrap it up," Ron said as he headed back into the restaurant.

"Are you sure you are up to coming back inside?" Karen asked.

Although I was grateful for Karen's concern, I was beginning to feel better, and Ron was right—it was definitely time to wrap it up. "Yes. Thanks." A little embarrassed by what had just occurred, I followed Karen inside.

By the time I reached the dining room, Ron Jr. was nearly done breaking down base camp.

Karen approached the team. She thumbed through her DR60, "Hey guys, I think I got something."

The room suddenly became quiet as we collectively gathered around her in anticipation.

She pressed the button on the recorder. My voice could be heard through the crackle of the speaker, "Did you die here?"

A voice not my own replied in a whispered rush, "Yes."

Instinctively, I looked to Margo to gauge her reaction and couldn't help but feel a slight vindication at the look on her face.

Karen played the recording several times. Each time the chatter in the room got louder.

Ron Jr. joined the group, "We're all packed up. Are we ready to go? I have to get up early tomorrow."

"Good idea," Ron responded as he turned toward Rick and extended his hand. "Thanks a lot."

"No. Thank you. It was great. I appreciate all your work tonight. It gave me a lot to think about. In fact," his lips turned up in a smile, *"what do you think about having a dinner here and presenting your findings?"*

"Great idea. I'll give you a call."

As we pulled away from Rick's, despite the evidence we collected, I couldn't help but think that the spirit had had the last laugh.

OUR THOUGHTS

MAUREEN:

It's very rare to encounter a physical altercation during a paranormal investigation. This investigation in particular produced a handful: rosary beads severed, lights turning on and off during the reading of St. Michael's prayer, and the zany digital numbers on the blood pressure cuff. Out of these, the severing of the rosary beads terrified me to no end. It wasn't just that they were severed, but the energy I felt and the force with which they were cut. It was a truly humbling experience that raised the hair on the back of my neck like nothing else.

RON:

Much as in the first episode, there was little physical evidence collected during the investigation. Without Maureen's insights, we had little to present. There did seem to be a relationship between the spirits and electrical devices such as the light going off when Maureen read St. Michael's prayer and the blood pressure cuff almost killing her. It also made me realize that although Rick's had reported numerous paranormal activities, it doesn't mean that we can dial it up on command. On a side note, after we did a dinner event there, a New Hampshire police officer contacted us and asked us to help with a cold case. Sometimes things do happen for a reason.

The Legend of Dudley Road

Case File: 1905874 The Legend of Dudley Road

Location: Billerica, Massachusetts

History: A long twisting two-lane road in Billerica running from Concord Road to Pine Hill Road. According to several urban legends, reported to be haunted by nuns.

Reported Paranormal Activity: There are many legends associated with Dudley Road, including escaped patients from an insane asylum, murdered nuns, houses sinking into the ground, and a car driving by itself.

Clients: N/A.

Investigators: Ron (lead investigator), Maureen (trance medium).

Press: N/A.

Purpose of Investigation: To explore the legend of Dudley Road.

Over the whirl of the AC in the car, Maureen spoke up, "Oh oh, Ron, I got to tell you. We got the uncorrected copies of *The Ghost Chronicles*, right."

"Yup."

"Well, I brought a copy to show my mother as we were driving on this two-hour escapade to my uncle's funeral. And get this, my mother tells me she wants to bring it in the church and the funeral parlor." She paused for emphasis. "Tell me, who in their right mind brings a copy of a book about talking with the dead into a church full of your relatives?"

"She's just proud of her little girl."

"She might be proud, but I tell her, 'Ma, NO!' So, what does she do?"

"What?"

"We are parked in a row at the funeral parlor waiting to go to the cemetery. She rolls down the window, and because she's half deaf, she starts yelling at my uncle who's parked across from us. 'Hey . . . Maureen and Ron just wrote a book about the dead!'"

"I replied, 'Ma, would you mind?'" She continued, "If that wasn't bad enough, she started all over again at the mercy meal."

Maureen and I burst out laughing.

"After four hundred yards, turn left," the digital voice of the GPS commanded.

"That English voice on your GPS is driving me crazy."

"Does this look like the road?" I asked Maureen.

"How do I know? I have never been here before."

"Turn left," the GPS intoned.

"I'm turning left!" I screamed, as the tires on my car squealed in response to my sharp turn.

"Oh, my God. Did you just learn how to use your breaks, Ron?"

"Oh, shut up. I am sure the guy behind me appreciated it."

"Yeah, I'm sure he did," Maureen responded, her voice thick with sarcasm.

"Nimwit. Can we turn that air conditioner down? I got icicles on my nose."

"It's not even on."

"Yes, it is all the way on."

Maureen studied the controls. "Oops. It's the opposite of mine."

"Does this look like a freakin' Audi?"

"Ah, no. Not even close." She laughed.

"Look at the bright side. I saved your car, 'cause this road ain't too good."

"You mean it is a little bumpy?"

"Could be. One of the things we're going to try is to let the steering wheel go and let the car drive by itself."

"Really?" Maureen laughed again. "Then I'm glad we took your car."

"Got your seat belt on?"

"I don't mind. I am in the passenger's seat," Maureen said, even as she buckled herself in.

"They call it the death seat, you know. . . ."

"Ha-ha-ha. Do you even know where you are going?"

Before I could respond, my English-accented GPS chimed in, "In two hundred yards, you have reached your destination."

"I am sooo done listening to her!" Maureen said in an irritated voice.

"Here we are. Dudley Road. Look, see that sign." Pointing to the right, I said, "Daughters of Saint Paul."

"Are you sure this is it?" Maureen said.

"I am not sure. What does that little sign say?"

Maureen squinted, "I don't know. From here, I can just see a skull and crossbones."

"Okay. Let's see if the car will drive itself." I took my hands off the wheel.

"Ah, Ron! It's not doing it." Maureen's voice grew louder. "Ron!"

Before we left the road, I grabbed the wheel.

"You know stories like this make you wonder how much is truth and how much is fiction and how much having your wheels aligned makes a difference," Maureen grumbled.

"So, here we are on Dudley Road. It's dark. It's scary. And look, Mom, no hands! And the car is driving down the middle of the road."

"Wait. Please turn right. Turn right, Ron. Please turn right. RON!"

I grasped the wheel for the second time. "Okay, maybe it doesn't work. Well, it did for about ten feet, anyway." I chuckled. "Just curious. Are you feeling anything, Maureen?"

"Besides the feeling you are going to get us killed?" she said as she breathed a deep sigh of relief. "I did feel like the atmosphere changed when we were going down the road."

"Okay, let's turn around and head back," I said as I stopped the car and did a U-turn.

This time as we traveled down the narrow country road, we heard a loud scraping noise.

"What the hell was that?" I asked.

"That was some tree limbs reaching out and scratching your car. Sure glad we didn't take the Audi." Maureen started to laugh, then stopped almost immediately. "Okay, right here. Stop. I'm feeling something now." Her voice wavered. "I am getting a really odd feeling right here."

Maureen cleared her throat repeatedly. "It actually feels like my throat's tight. Like it is being restricted."

"Anything else?" I asked, pressing for more information.

"It seems a little odd, but I feel like someone is being beaten or killed by a group of people. It was a long time ago. Maybe two hundred years."

A thought occurred to me, "You know, this doesn't look good."

"What doesn't?"

"You and I sitting in a parked car, alone on a secluded road together . . ."

"Okay, clean up that mind of yours." As if experiencing an ah-ha moment, she added, "Maybe you're right. In that case, let's move a little farther down the road."

"Are you still picking up on anything?"

"No, it went away."

"All right, let's try something. Can you get me my EMF meter from the back seat?"

Maureen undid her seat belt, leaned back, stretching as far as she could. "Here it is."

I took the meter from Maureen and flipped the switch. "I'm going to put it on the dashboard to see if we pick up anything."

I turned back to Maureen. "Do you know anything about this place?"

"No not a thing," she replied. Then as if she wanted be anywhere but parked in one place, she said, "All right, let's drive again."

Several moments later, she added, "I know this sounds weird, but there's something about nuns and this place."

"Really? I'm listening."

"You are not going to like it."

"Why?"

"Because you're a good ol' religious boy."

"Do you want me to stop the car?"

A look of horror washed over her face. "No, because you said it might not look right."

"Oh, shut up. Like that has ever stopped us before." A thought crossed my mind, and I couldn't help myself. "Do I have to show you the picture from the psychomanteum chamber?"

PSYCHOMANTEUM CHAMBER

A small dark chamber used to facilitate communication with the spirits of the dead. Its roots date back to ancient Greece, but in its modern form, it was popularized by Dr. Raymond Moody. Dr. Moody is an award-winning author and the leading authority on near death experience—a phrase he coined in the 1970s.

"No!" she squealed. "And don't ever bring that up again."

"Fine. You're so touchy."

She hesitated for a moment, then continued, "Okay, I have no idea why I keep picking this up, but I see something about a nun and something about a 'loose woman.' A lady-of-the-night kind of woman. It keeps coming to me over and over again."

Once again, she took a moment to concentrate, then spoke, "I think it was a loose woman who became a nun. And there's more. I also got this feeling that there was a murder." Maureen grasped her throat when she spoke. "I don't know. Something to do with my throat."

"Your throat killed her?"

"You're such a jerk. It felt like a hanging. And I don't think there are any records on it. I feel it was done on the sly."

"Interesting." I thought for a moment, then said, "Let me ask you this. If there are spirits here, can they feed you false information?"

"Can they? As a matter of fact, I know that someone is."

"What does that mean?"

"I don't know. I might be picking up stuff from your head that you know is false."

"That would screw this whole experiment up," I said.

"It certainly would. Seriously. So, stop it." Maureen was getting agitated. "This is really weird. It feels like people's thoughts. But it doesn't feel real. And it's nothing I've ever felt before." Emphasizing her words, she finished, "It also feels like a cover-up. It doesn't make sense to me."

"Wait a minute. This reminds me of the Philip experiment."

"What is the Philip experiment? I've never heard of it."

I explained, "Back in 1970 or so, mathematician A. R. G. Owen and psychologist Dr. Joel Whitton created a ghost."

A quizzical look crossed her face. "What?"

"You heard me right. A ghost. They made up this haunted house story. They created his history, the legend of his haunting—the whole shebang. Then they held a séance with unsuspecting people and achieved what is believed communication with the ghost that never existed."

"Really? So they manifested it?"

"Yes. It seems so. In fact, I've been wondering if that's what you've been picking up."

A scraping noise coming from outside the car drew my attention. "What was that noise?"

"Branches on the car again." Maureen chuckled.

"Great. Jan's gonna love me."

"Hey, I'm feeling something right here. Pull over. Quick."

"Here?"

"Yes."

As the car came to a stop, Maureen muttered, "Okay, give me a minute."

Impatiently, I began pulling my pendulum out of my pocket. "If you don't want to dowse, then I will."

"Geez, Ron. I do want to do the pendulum. Give me a chance. It's not like flipping a switch, you know."

"All right, we're not going anywhere. Focus."

"I am," she said as she pulled out her own crystal pendulum.

"What, is that glass?"

"No. It's quartz."

"Yeah, right."

Speaking to the pendulum, Maureen began to ask questions. "Is Dudley Road haunted?"

The crystal spun counterclockwise, indicating yes.

I piped in, "How many spirits are here?"

The pendulum responded quickly, while Maureen continued her questioning. "Are there more than one, more than three? Are there five spirits here?"

Once again, the answer was a yes.

I asked, "Do they know the rumors about the haunting of Dudley Road?"

Maureen nodded. "Yes. Yes, they do."

I continued. "Do they play games with the people who come to look for them?"

The pendulum swung back and forth. She laughed out loud. "Sometimes."

"Is there any connection between my throat and what I am feeling and this area on Dudley Road?" Maureen said, clutching her throat with her free hand.

Yes.

"Is there an abandoned insane asylum off Dudley Road?" I asked.

"Yes, but you know what's funny? They are saying yes, but I don't feel there is."

I reaffirmed Maureen's thoughts. "There is no record of one."

"Then who the hell is messin' with us?"

"Are you telling us what we want hear?"

Yes.

Maureen frowned. "Well, isn't that just ducky?!"

I grumbled. "So it looks like we're not going to get anything useful from them, are we?"

Maureen continued asking the pendulum questions: "Has anyone been hung by a tree on Dudley Road? Are there any spirits of dead nuns that haunt here? Was she a loose woman before she became a nun?" Each and every question we asked resulted in the same response: yes. As if the puzzle pieces began to fit, Maureen gasped. "Is that a story, Ron?"

"Yes, these are all stories. All part of the legend of Dudley Road. And, by the way, none of them are true."

"Really? You guys aren't being nice." Maureen placed her hand to her temple and concentrated. Then she said, "Oh, my God. They're laughing. I can hear laughter."

Putting my hand to my chest, I could feel the heaviness setting in—a sure sign to me that there was spirit around. "I feel it, too."

Maureen raised her arm toward me. "Look! The hairs on my arms are standing up. There is definitely something here. I'm going to try and get beneath the façade."

"Good luck," I said, as I thought to myself, *With the results we're getting, you'll need it.*

"Yeah, I know it," Maureen replied as she lowered her head into her hands.

"What are you doing? You going deep?"

"Yup."

"She's going down. Oops, never mind . . ."

She screeched, "Oh, my God. Stop it!"

I could feel the heat on my face. "I'm sorry. That's not what I meant. Forget what I said."

"Like I could."

"Come on, focus. Get serious." Even though I was telling her to focus, I couldn't believe what had just came out of my mouth. *I really need to start thinking before I speak.*

The laughter of just a moment ago dissipated, while Maureen's voice took on a serious tone. "Okay, um, I'm getting something. So, this is very strange and doesn't make sense to me."

"Go ahead," I prodded.

"While the energy appears to be a man or a woman, it seems more like something that was never a man or a woman. Do you know what I mean?"

"Demonic?" I asked, not really wanting to hear the answer.

"No, more of an earth energy, and I hate to say it, but it seems to get off on all these games it plays. Now, this is weird, but I am seeing a well around here and someone working with herbs and spices." Maureen shook her head and gasped. "Who's messing with me?"

I laughed. "That's another rumor."

"What?" She replied in disbelief.

"Yes. Somebody dealing with witchcraft. You have mentioned every rumor associated with this place."

"I am getting the name Beladon."

"Write it down."

"I can't even spell it," Maureen grumbled. "What the heck? I want to say it is some kind of drug or something that was used in witchcraft. Beladream, belladonna. It doesn't make sense, but I keep hearing it in my head over and over. It is some chemical used in witchcraft. Years and years and years ago when I was eighteen, I was involved in Wicca." She looked up as if to see my reaction. "Well, it wasn't *that* long ago."

"Yeah, in your mind."

"I used to do witchcraft, but I can't remember this name."

"I know Beltane is a Wiccan holiday."

"No. That's not it. I hear it over and over again like a rhyme," she said, as she made revolving motions with her hand. "A rhythmic thing."

"A chant?"

"Yes, that's it." She continued on. "I can see them taking some kind of roots and herbs and something. It is bizarre for me because it is like a hallucinogen. It is like they are messing with my head."

"Okay, but they're still playing mind games."

Maureen released an exasperated sigh, "Yup, but I'm still getting something about a loose woman who became a nun."

"Well, maybe that's what they want you to see."

"That may be very possible, but I can't control that right now." Maureen grimaced. "I'm getting a pain in my chest."

"Where? In the center?"

"Yes." Maureen took a moment to catch her breath. "They are saying everybody wants to know." She closed her eyes as if to concentrate on what she was hearing. After a moment she said, "I don't get it. 'Know' what?"

With the last of Maureen's words, a thought popped into my mind. "Do they try to trick the ghost hunters who come here looking to find the legends?" I asked.

"Yes," she said.

"Did they die on this road?"

"No. They didn't die here. They lived here. They held some kind of ceremony here."

Unable to control my aggravation, I responded, "Geez. How do we know they aren't lying to us now?"

"We can't. I can only tell you what I'm getting."

"Can't you make them tell the truth? Evoke somebody or something?"

"I don't know. They could just possibly walk away or slither away. Oops, sorry about that."

Surprised by her uncharacteristic response, I said, "That was mean."

"Sorry about that. I was just kidding," she groaned with a halfhearted apology.

I grew more agitated. "Tell them we command them to only tell us the truth."

"They want to know, 'Whose truth?'"

"God's truth."

Maureen snapped. "No. There is no God here." Her eyes grew wide, "What does that tell you."

"Yikes, look at my arm!" I said, extending my arm out in front of Maureen. "My hair is standing straight up."

"Oh, boy." Maureen jerked as her body involuntarily shivered. "Eww. I just saw a whole bunch of black slithery snakes. That's disgusting."

"Now this is weird. I'm not a psychic, but I can see some dark primitive figures standing around a fire."

"You know what, Ron? They might be druids, not witches," Maureen said as she rested her head back, suddenly looking drawn as if the last few moments had drained the life from her.

"Okay, I've had enough of these jokers. Let's get out of the car. Let's go over to that retreat building."

The car doors slammed behind us, and we approached the chain-link fence that surrounded the building. I turned back toward Maureen. "Are you feeling anything here?"

"Just that same strange kind of dark, oppressive feeling. You know, I don't think I should feel it just outside a religious retreat though."

"Why?"

"I don't know. I just think I would feel more peace and tranquility outside a religious retreat than these bizarre feelings."

"Well, we are not inside. Aren't there boundaries?"

"Yeah, you're right."

Apparently ready to call it a night, she began, "Well, it's been an interesting trip here to Dudley Road. I've received various snippets of information. But I can't tell what truth is versus the crap they're feeding me. All I know is that I have never been to Dudley Road. And I can say that it is an uncomfortable feeling being down here, and I don't particularly care for it. Right now, I can't help but wonder if all these people who live in these houses along this road have seen or experienced anything."

"Well, there is a house across the street. We could go up and knock on their door and ask them." I laughed out loud. "However, I don't think they would take too kindly to strangers knocking on the door in the middle of the night."

"No, I don't think that would fly very well."

"Speaking about flying, isn't that a cop car?" I said looking at the blue lights getting closer by the minute. "Maybe it is time *we* better fly out of here. . . ."

OUR THOUGHTS

MAUREEN:

I like to approach being a medium as an ongoing opportunity to learn. This was one investigation that taught me plenty. For instance, it reinforced my belief that as we are energy, so are our thoughts. And perhaps the numerous legends attached to Dudley Road were piled atop each other, layered like an energetic cake—a cake that lay in wait for those sensitive enough to cut in and engorge themselves on a fantastical, morbid bite.

RON:

What started out as an experiment in dealing with urban legends turned into a lesson in the psychology of spirit. Judging from what we could uncover that day, we determined that spirits do not always tell the truth and seemingly can be who you wish them to be. Do they feed off our fears, thoughts, emotions, and preconceived notions, manipulating us for their own purpose? Or is there something more sinister afoot?

The 1859 House

Case File: 1905432 1859 House

Location: Methuen, Massachusetts

History: The original building was built in 1859 by the Methuen Company, a textile manufacturer. It was leased and eventually purchased by the Methuen Club, composed of a group of local and professional men. The private club became a mecca for its members, providing them with a pub-style bar, bowling alleys in the basement, and an array of billiard and card tables on the upper levels. It was even rumored that the members were entertained by women of the night there. The movers and shakers of Methuen met there to plot and discuss the future of the town. Eventually, the club dissolved and the building was sold and later turned into a restaurant.

Reported Paranormal Activity: Dark shadow in the basement, objects moving by themselves, cold spots, visitors to the restaurant report seeing the spirit of a woman in the ladies' room.

Clients: John and Hope Zahos.

Investigators: Ron (lead investigator), Maureen (trance medium), Ron Jr. (investigator), Karen (EVP specialist), Jim (photographer).

Press: N/A.

Purpose of Investigation: Public ghost-hunting event.

As Maureen and I finished our dinner in the old English pub atmosphere of the 1859 House, I saw two young ladies approaching our table—Nancy and Joy. They were two of the participants from the first half of this event, which was held at Circles of Wisdom, a metaphysical store in Andover, Massachusetts. I thought it a bit odd that two spiritualists from Salem, Massachusetts, would join us for a ghost-hunting event, since they deal with spirits all the time.

"Hi, Ron and Maureen," Joy said with a big grin.

"Hello, ladies. Ready for the ghost hunt?"

"Are we ever?! I can't tell you enough how much we enjoyed last night's seminar."

"So what do you think of tonight's location?"

"I can tell you, Ron, I felt the energy of several spirits as soon as I walked in. Don't you agree, Maureen?"

"Absolutely. You should check out the bathroom and let me know what you think."

Joy gave a quick nod. Barely able to contain the smile on her face, she grabbed Nancy by the arm. "Let's go."

"Okay. We'll see you in a little bit." I turned to Maureen. "You sent them to the bathroom?"

She started laughing. "What? You forget the first night we met in person? Don't you remember you sent me to the ladies' room?"

"Yeah, so?"

"Did you think I didn't know you were testing my mediumship abilities? Then when I came back, you gave me the third degree."

"I have no idea what you're talking about." *I lied.*

"Yeah, right. Remember, I'm psychic." Maureen chuckled.

The radio crackled as Ron Jr.'s voice came through. "Dad, we're all set up here. People are starting to file in. You guys better get up here."

"Roger. We'll be right up."

It was now seven o'clock and time to rock. "Okay, everybody, before we get started, we're going to play you a video of our first investigation here. The one that aired on WNDS."

Later, as the last of the credits rolled, Ron Jr. turned up the lights.

"All right, any questions before we start?" I said

From the back of the room, the hand of a tall fellow shot up. "As you know, I'm from the AA-EVP. Are we going to have an opportunity to do EVPs tonight?"

AA-EVP (AMERICAN ASSOCIATION OF ELECTRONIC VOICE PHENOMENON)

Group founded by Sarah Estep in 1982 as her way of helping people learn about and experiment with EVP.

"Of course. Karen, who's also an AA-EVP member, is in charge of that.

"Any other questions?"

From the front row, a young woman spoke up, "After watching that video, me and my boyfriend are a little freaked out here. Is there any way we can protect ourselves?"

Maureen stepped to the front of the room and said, "Yes. There are numerous ways to protect yourself. Having faith in whatever you believe in is the first step. You can also use various items. For instance, I carry around crystals and coins. Not sure if you are aware, but metal can be grounding."

I interjected, "Of course, being a good ol' Catholic boy, I always use holy water, my St. Michael's prayer, and of course, Van Helsing's special blend.

VAN HELSING'S SPECIAL BLEND

A spiritual cleansing spray developed by Ron. It comes in a Reiki-infused bottle with a St. Michael's prayer card printed on the label and a blessed silver cross attached.

"Thanks for reminding me. By the way, for those interested, I have a bottle of each on the table in the back. You're welcome to use it," I said.

"Okay. Before we begin, I'd like to introduce someone special who's with us tonight. His name is Dan Parsons, and he's a deputy fire chief. He's brought with him tonight a thermal imager." I gestured to a man who resembled the lumberjack from the Brawny paper towel commercial. "Dan, would you mind coming up here and telling us a little about it?"

Dan's eyes grew wide. "Ah, sure. I guess I can do that."

He rose from his seat and made his way through the crowd, carrying a black handheld device that looked like a futuristic speed gun. He held it at arm's length while he used his free hand to point to the large screen on the imager. "What you're looking at now is the various thermal images of this wall. Ron, can you go and put your hand on the wall, please?"

"Sure." I hurried over and placed my hand on the cool plaster. "Like this?"

"Yeah. That's good. Now take your hand off and walk away from the wall."

The crowd gasped as the thermal image of my hand remained on the wall, even though I had removed it.

"Wow, that's cool." I took a look at the crowd. They were getting antsy and I knew we had to get going, so I said, "Okay. Thanks, Dan. Now, let's get this show on the road.

"Last night we taught you how to use dowsing rods and EMF meters. We have some of them on the back table over there, if you'd like to try them out." I'd almost forgotten. "Oh yeah, if you want to use any holy water or special blend, it's over there." I said, pointing to another table off to the right.

A familiar yelp resounded from the back of the room. I looked to see Joy picking herself up off the floor. I rushed to her side. "Are you all right? What happened?"

As she dusted off her knees, she said, "You're not going to believe this. I think I just got pushed by a spirit."

"Really? I hope you're okay." I couldn't help but think, *This is a sign of things to come.*

"If you're okay, then let's get going."

Within minutes, I could barely hear my own thoughts above the thumping and creaking of the old wooden steps as the twenty-three-odd people ascended the stairs to the third floor.

We walked down a long, narrow hallway and entered the last room on the right. The room was in disrepair. The wallpaper, old and peeling, showed us a glimpse of what the Methuen club had once looked like. "We'll start here."

Maureen, pendulum in hand, began to make contact with the spirits. "This is crazy, Ron. We just walked in, and I can feel the energy already." She hesitated as if to gather her thoughts. "Okay. So, I'm picking up on three spirits. There's a man. A woman. And a little girl."

"Did they die here?"

She cried out in pain as she reached up and began rubbing the back of her head. "Ow, my head!" She pulled her hand off her head and inspected her hand. "What the hell? I felt like I was hit in the head. It feels so real, I thought I was bleeding." She pressed her hand to her head again. "Unreal. I think he just showed me how he died. He was murdered. A blow to the back of the head."

"Why don't we give Maureen a break for a minute," I continued. "Everyone, let's break up into teams and fan out to begin your own investigation. Please stay on this floor."

Dan called out from one of the other rooms, "Ron, come here for a minute."

I followed the sound of his voice. Upon entering the room, I spotted Dan and his shaman friend standing beside what appeared to be an old closet. "What's going on?"

Dan held out his thermal imager and said, "We saw this small gray shape, and it disappeared into this closet."

His friend spoke up, "I think it might be the little girl that Maureen was talking about."

"Did you look inside, you clunker heads?"

Dan laughed. "No. We waited for you."

I walked over to the closet door, grabbed the rusted metal door knob, and gave it a yank. Much to my dismay, it was empty.

Dan continued to scan the room. "Ron, look. Over there."

EMF meter in hand, I walked to where Dan had pointed and slowly lowered my meter. A short distance from the floor, the meter began to blare as its red light illuminated the room.

The next few minutes I spent chasing this apparition throughout the fourth floor until I felt an odd sensation begin to whisk around my lower legs. "You know. This is weird, Dan. I think it's a cat."

"You're right. Look at it," he said, pointing once again to the screen. "Look right here. There's an outline and what looks like a tail. Oh, my God. It *is* a cat!"

Soon, my meter went dead, and with it, the image was no longer visible. "Well, that was cool. I'm going to go check on Maureen," I said as I walked out the door.

When I found Maureen, she was in light conversation with Joy and Nancy. She turned when she heard me enter. "Ron, you're not going to believe this, but I just picked up on a cat of all things. That's a first."

"Did you just say cat? Dan just saw one on the thermal imager a little while ago. Isn't that so cool?"

Ron Jr.'s voice once again crackled over the radio. "Time's up. You've got to move on to the next location."

"Okay, we're heading to the basement."

I followed Ron back down the stairs until we reached a big heavy door with two large slide-bolt locks that led to the basement. I stood back as Ron yanked on the door and thought to myself, Were the bolts on the door there to keep someone out or someone or something in? *I had a strange feeling I'd soon find out.*

Sinking into the darkness, we descended the stairs to the basement, an area that the employees dubbed "the dungeon."

"Which way, Ron?"

"Let's go to the left. That's where we got that great photograph of that black cloud in the previous investigation."

"That was before my time."

"Yes, it was. In fact, I think Brian, the monk, was with us. So, I guess you don't remember the bowling alley. They still had a chalkboard on the wall with the final scores of the last game that was played here."

BRIAN, THE MONK

A Franciscan monk who taught Ron the art of infrared photography. Maureen and Ron accompanied Brian to assist a woman and her dog who were being tormented by a demon in an old Victorian townhouse. Together, they performed an exorcism to free this woman from her demonic stalker, as described in Episode Six of their first book, *The Ghost Chronicles*.

"*That's pretty cool,*" *one of the attendees said.*

Once we'd all piled into the left-hand side of the basement, Karen took the group of AA-EVP members to the concrete slab to the right to see if they could capture any EVPs.

While we waited for the remainder of the attendees to huddle around us, I closed my eyes to see if I could connect with the energy swirling about me. Sometimes it takes a minute to get focused. As I stood amidst the group, the energy came closer, growing even stronger. But something felt odd. It was as if whoever or whatever was with us had begun taunting me, giving me a glimpse of its presence but pulling back just as quickly.

Ron, frantically waving his meter in the air, addressed the group. "I'm not picking up anything. Is anyone else?" He scanned the group and noticed through his disappointment that there was no response. He turned once again to me, in frustration, and said, "I'm not picking up on anything."

Although the crystal of my pendulum began to spin wildly, I really didn't need it. I knew the spirit was here. I could feel its anger amplifying by the minute. "Ron, I'm telling you. It's here."

Ron continued to scan air about us. "Look. I've got nothing." He pointedly scanned the room, then back at me. "None of us do."

"I'm telling you, Ron. It's here." With the last of my words, I instinctively knew why the meters hadn't picked up on it. It was playing with us. Staying just out of reach as it continued to swirl above our heads. "Ron, it's above us."

He raised the meter at arm's length above his head, and it began to blare. "You're right," he said as the red light, instead of blinking, was nearly continuous. "Can you connect with him?"

"Not really. He's staying out of reach."

Ron grew impatient. "Well, reel him in."

Without even my thinking, Ron's words entered my mind. The entity, taking it as an invitation, pounced at the opportunity.

I watched Ron's hand as he followed the entity that sped toward me. I shuddered.

I pushed back and repelled the onslaught of energy that attempted to enter me.

For now I stood my ground.

A split second later it hit me again.

This time, stronger.

Harder.

I was unable to repel it. It surged through my body.

My knees buckled.

I plummeted to the ground.

My backside hit the cold, damp, dirt floor beneath me.

As if I was standing outside my body, I could hear a guttural voice coming from my own lips, "The bitch. The bitch, die. My life."

This was my body, and I was damned determined not to allow this angry spirit to use it.

With all the strength I could muster, I shoved back again, pushing the entity out of my body and back to where it came.

Ron dropped his equipment and rushed to me. I sat on the ground, unable to even lift my arms to raise myself off. "Are you all right?" Ron asked.

Although it was a short encounter, it drained every ounce of energy from me. So much so, I was finding it hard to even speak.

Joy, Nancy, and their friend Todd rushed to my side. "Maureen, don't move. We're here to help," Joy said as all three of them laid their hands on my shoulder and back.

Still unable to speak, I barely nodded my head in agreement. It was enough. They then began performing Reiki upon my depleted body.

REIKI

A Japanese healing technique based on the channeling of energy. The word *Reiki* comes from the Japanese word (*Rei*), which means "universal life" and (*Ki*), which means "energy."

As the crowd grew louder, Ron spoke up, "Ron Jr., take the group up to the third floor to continue the investigation. I'm going to help Maureen outside."

"Okay, Dad." Ron Jr. hesitated, then turned to address the group, "Okay, people. Follow me."

As the last thump of the footsteps ascended the stairs, Ron grabbed my arm and helped me off the floor. "Okay, Maureen. Why don't we go outside and get some fresh air?"

Moments later we stood together in the cool, crisp, night air, under a lamppost in front of the 1859 House. My legs still shaking beneath me, I wagged my finger at Ron. "Don't ever say, 'Reel it in' again."

"Whatever. Did you get a sense for who or what that spirit was?"

"Yeah. It was the guy we communicated with upstairs. Don't you remember? He said, 'I'll see you in the basement.' I think it's because that's where his energy is the strongest.

"I get the feeling he was murdered, hit on the back of the head by a lady of the night. You know—a prostitute."

"Really?"

"Yeah, I have a feeling that when it was the Methuen club, they used their services."

"Why do you think she killed him?"

"She was jealous. She loved him, only to be rebuked. Killing him in a jealous rage."

"That's interesting. So what the hell was he so pissed off about?"

"She took his life and got away with it. Wouldn't you be pissed off?"

"Yeah, that would be irritating."

The restaurant door opened wide as Ron Jr. poked his head out. "Oh, there you are. We're all finished investigating. Do you want to wrap it up?"

"Yeah. We'll be right in."

Ron looked at me and said, "You ready to go back in, Kid."

"If I must."

As we said our good-byes to the guests, I couldn't help but notice the looks I got, let alone the few who purposely sidestepped, trying to avoid me.

Instinctively, I knew this was a night that few would forget.

OUR THOUGHTS

MAUREEN:

The 1859 House investigation left an impression on my psyche that will forever remain. Like each and every paranormal contact with spirit, it feels that I have been given one more piece to a cosmic puzzle. This little piece of the puzzle? The reaffirmation that not all spirits play by the same set of rules, proving that just because an EMF meter or other piece of mechanical equipment is not picking up on a presence does not indicate the lack of spiritual communication. Oh, and one other thing, to make sure that Ron never says, "Reel 'em in" ever again!

RON:

Although this was a "ghost-hunting event," we obtained some interesting results. On the upper floor, I had the strange sensation that I was being rubbed up against by a cat but could see nothing. However, the thermal imager revealed the image of what appeared to be a ghost cat. This was intriguing. In the basement, my request for Maureen to reel the spirit in for the sake of the crowd showed poor judgment, causing Maureen great discomfort and scaring some of the participants. I learned a painful lesson (more Maureen than me) that when dealing with the spirit world and the unknown, it is no joking matter.

The Portsmouth Harbor Lighthouse

Case File: 194976 Portsmouth Harbor Lighthouse

Location: New Castle, New Hampshire

History: The station was built in 1771 and was the tenth lighthouse station established prior to the American Revolution. In 1804, the original tower was replaced by an eighty-foot octagonal wooden tower. In 1851, the tower was shortened to fifty-five feet. Three years later, the tower was fitted with a Fourth Order Fresnel lens. In 1878, a new forty-eight-foot cast iron brick-lined tower was erected on the same foundation of the 1804 tower. The adjacent oil house was built in 1903.

Reported Paranormal Activity: Disembodied voices, apparitions.

Clients: Roxie Zwicker, Jeremy D'Entremont.

Investigators: Ron (lead investigator), Maureen (trance medium), Ron Jr. (investigator), Dan Parsons, Jim (photographer), Karen (EVP specialist), St. Jan (Ron's wife).

Press: Scott and sound man (filmmaker).

Purpose of Investigation: To try to explain the strange occurrences at the lighthouse, Coast Guard base, and Fort Constitution.

Sipping my coffee, I savored the black liquid, eagerly anticipating the familiar rush of energy while I waited for my computer to boot. Never was a morning person. Thank God for caffeine.

After what felt like hours but couldn't have been more than a matter of a few moments, the screen came alive. I clicked on the envelope icon on my desktop and sighed when it came into view. A sea of unopened emails stared back at me. Guess it was going to be one of those days.

Not in the mood to deal with the umpteenth piece of spam mail, I nearly deleted the next message on impulse, until I spied a familiar name: Roxie Zwicker. If memory served, she was an author and historian and the proprietor of New England Curiosities ghost tours. Intrigued, I clicked on the message.

Hey Ron—Long time no chat. I meant to contact you earlier, but it's been so busy around here that I'd almost forgot. It's about investigating the Lighthouse. I spoke with Jeremy and the Coast Guard station and they're good with it. Can you call me to schedule a time when you guys can come out to investigate? The sooner the better.

Thanks,
Roxie

Sensing the immediacy and eager to have the opportunity to investigate the lighthouse, I contacted Roxie and set up the meeting.

———·—

Two weeks later we arrived outside the gate of the Coast Guard station, where we were met by Roxie and Jeremy. After a brief meeting, Roxie addressed the group. "All right, everyone. It's a bit far to walk to the lighthouse, especially lugging equipment. So, if you wouldn't mind following Jeremy and I, we'll show you the way."

Single file, we drove through the gate. Gravel crunched beneath the tires as the car bounced and rattled down the wind-swept dirt road. Several minutes later we passed the Coast Guard station and arrived at the lighthouse. Salt air assailed my senses the second I stepped out of the car. I took a deep breath and breathed in deeply the rich salt air. With daylight waning and a big night of investigating ahead, we quickly dragged our equipment into the lighthouse and set up base camp.

As I knelt down and busily worked on setting up the wires for the base camp monitor, someone tapped on my shoulder. "Hi, are you Ron?"

"Yes," I said as I scrambled to my feet and turned to see two burly men in uniform standing in front of the door.

The taller of the two extended his hand. "I'm Matt, and this guy here is Jonathon." He grinned like there was a silent joke going on between them.

I shook their hands. "Nice to meet you."

"Same here. We have something we'd like to share with you if you have time to listen."

"Sure, I always have time for the boys in blue."

"Well, I know this might sound a little strange." Matt glanced to Jonathon and then back to me and then continued, "Late at night, when we're in the control tower monitoring the base, we often see the figure of a woman in white walking atop the sea walls and the walls surrounding the fort. When we go to investigate, she disappears." I turned to look for Maureen. She was nowhere in sight. Good. As a rule, we don't listen to stories before an investigation for fear of tainting the information she gives us.

Matt continued, "We don't like talking about this stuff. We're not quite sure what to think about it." He hesitated for a moment as if he was unsure of what to say next. "I'll tell ya, some of the guys won't go into the fort at night."

"Wow. That's interesting." I had a thought. "You know, you're welcome to stay for the investigation."

They looked from one to another, then back to me. "No thanks. We're good." They left.

With that, I turned to the rest of the group and said, "Has anyone seen Maureen?" As if she heard me call her name, she walked into the lighthouse.

"When are you going to start this thing? It's getting cold out here."

"Whine, whine, whine," I laughed. "All right, let's get going."

Jeremy spoke up, "Do you want to go to the top first?"

"Sure," I replied.

Taking the lead, Jeremy led the group up the narrow winding metal stairs of the lighthouse. As I reached the fourth step, it was as if I bounced off an invisible wall.

Ron Jr. bumped into the back of me. "What's that all about?"

"I don't know. It felt like something pushed me back."

"Okay. This should be a good night."

———·—·———

As I heard Ron's voice echo from the bottom of the stairs, I began to feel the first stirrings of energy. To investigate further, I stopped at one of the small windows that peered out over the moonlit sea. Suddenly, a strange feeling came over me.

The overwhelming presence of woman overtook me.

Like a hand slipping into a glove, I no longer felt I was wearing my worn-out jeans; instead, I was wearing her long, flowing skirt. Mesmerized, I caught myself gazing out the window and searching the horizon. For what? I do not know. I was suddenly overcome with emotion as a tear rolled down my cheek.

"What's the holdup?" Ron bellowed from below.

So into my thoughts, I was finding it difficult to respond. So unlike me. Taking his cue, I continued upstairs. As if still wearing the spirit's skirt, I found myself suddenly having the urge to lift the hem of the dress as I gingerly walked each step.

At the top of the stairs, we all entered a small room with brass portholes.

As the last of us entered the room, his lordship spoke up, "Karen, why don't you try some EVPs while Maureen dowses."

I pulled out my pendulum and began to dowse. "Is there someone here with us now?" The pendulum slowly rotated clockwise. Yes. "Are you a female?" This time the pendulum rotated counterclockwise. No.

"Ron, I know the pendulum's working, but I can barely sense the energy."

Ron turned to Karen. "Okay, Karen, why don't you try a couple EVPs?"

Karen turned on her recorder and began, "Is there anyone here that wants to speak with us?"

Silence filled the room as we waited patiently for the spirit to respond.

"Are you a male?" Karen paused. "Can you tell us your name?"

"Karen, did you get anything?" Ron asked.

Karen snapped back, "I'll let you know in a minute."

Fiddling with the recorder, Karen hit play. Her voice echoed through the recorder with no reply to the first two questions. When it reached the part where she'd asked for the spirit to tell her their name, a faint voice replied. She increased the volume and played it again. This time, a raspy voice could be heard through the tiny speaker: "The Captain."

Jeremy gasped. "Did I hear what I think I heard? Did it just say, 'The Kaptain?'"

Karen stood up straighter and pushed the hair from her face. "Sure sounds like it to me."

"You're not gonna believe this, but Joshua Card, the longest-serving lighthouse keeper here, used to go by that name. People would ask him what the K stood for on his uniform; he would respond, 'Kaptain.'"

We stood there for a few moments longer. Unable to get any more results, we decided to make our way back down.

As we descended the stairs, Thermal Dan's voice echoed from outside the lighthouse. "Ron, come here quick!"

I ran past Maureen, down the stairs, and out the door, where Dan was standing with the thermal imager. "Check this out."

As I peered into the screen, there seemed to be the image of a man standing by a small brick building, which was the oil house. But looking up, I could see there was no one there. We kept our eyes fixed on the shadowy image, only to have him disappear when we approached the spot where he stood.

Behind me, I heard the clamor of footsteps on the walkway as the team closed in on us.

"What happened?" Ron Jr. asked.

Dan lifted the imager as if to show everyone what had occurred, but the screen was blank. "We had this figure on it, standing here. But as we approached, it . . . it just disappeared."

Turning the corner, we entered the door of the oil house. One by one we filed in to fill the tiny space. We stood in a circle. Without saying a word, Maureen reached into her pocket and withdrew her pendulum. She inhaled deeply and closed her eyes.

With Ron by my side, the tingle of energy that I'd felt before, when I first walked in, was growing stronger by the minute—a sign that a spirit was present and eager to communicate. I held the pendulum in my hand and began asking questions of our unseen visitor.

"Is there someone here that wants to speak with us?"

The pendulum responded in a yes.

Suddenly, I felt a shift. My face felt as if it was being twisted and contorted. Disfigured. Burned beyond recognition.

I looked around the room, the blank stares an indication that no one could see what I was feeling. I knew now that it was no longer my face, but that of the spirit. It felt so real, I brushed my hand against my cheek to be sure. Now reassured, I turned to Ron and said, "I feel as if I've been in a fire. An explosion."

"Were you a soldier?" Jeremy asked.

Unsure, I tightened my grip on the pendulum and repeated Jeremy's question.

Yes.

Jeremy continued, "Did you die here?"

Again, the pendulum responded with a yes.

Ron spoke up, "Does anyone smell smoke?"

Everyone collectively sniffed the air about them. If it wasn't such a serious moment, I would have laughed out loud.

Through a chorus of yesses, I felt the energy wane. Our newly found friend was departing.

"I think he's gone."

The look of disappointment washed over Jeremy's face. "He's gone?"

"Well, he ain't here anymore," Ron quipped.

Jeremy continued, "Well, there was an accident at the fort. Ten people were killed. One was actually blown over here to the lighthouse."

Ron chimed in, "Well, let's go to the fort then."

Within a few moments, the oil house was behind us as we trekked through the entrance of the sally port.

SALLY PORT

A secured entranceway into a fortification or prison. It allows troops to exit when making a sally (skirmish).

After visiting the lookout tower and gun and placement with few results, we entered the powder magazine, the oldest structure in the fort.

Like the numbers on a clock face, we stood facing each other. I still held my pendulum at the ready. Standing in the oldest building, I half expected to feel something. My high expectations were quickly replaced by disappointment. However, as the group began chatting among themselves, the space in the room began to feel crowded. We were no longer by ourselves. Our friend from the oil house had returned. "He's back."

"Who? How can you tell?" Thermal Dan asked.

"After so many years of doing this, I've come to realize that each spirit's energy has its own unique signature."

"Do you know his name?" Jeremy asked.

With Jeremy's question, the energy grew in strength. Concentrating, I closed my eyes, waiting for the spirit to come closer. As I gained his confidence, his name began to materialize in my mind. Taking a leap of faith, I began to verbalize. "Daniel?" I hesitated. "Yes, I think that's it. Daniel."

"I don't have the list of those that died in the explosion," Jeremy said. "But I'll look it up later."

Just then, I felt a sudden pull to leave. Barely able to speak, I walked passed everyone and out the door of the magazine. As if being led, I began walking across the courtyard. The brisk night air caressing my face. I glanced up as I walked and gasped at the expanse of stars overhead. It was truly magical. I continued walking until I reached the fort's wall. Once there, not to waste the moment, I stared out of the gun port at the breaking waves. In mere seconds, I felt Daniel's presence. An overwhelming sorrow surged through my body. I began to cry.

Jeremy walked up beside me. "Are you okay?"

I found myself speaking through sobs. "He feels guilty. There was some kind of celebration." I reached into my pocket and pulled out a tissue and blotted the mascara that I knew had to be running down my face. I continued, "He's sorry. It's not his fault."

"Maureen, why don't you take a break for a minute while I try an EVP?" Karen said as she clutched her recorder.

Jeremy, familiar with Karen's routine, spoke into the recorder. "Do you know it's not your fault?"

Karen asked a few more questions, then listened to the playback. Through the static she heard Jeremy's voice, "Do you know it's not your fault?" There was a slight pause and then a distinct reply, "Yes."

It seems that Daniel had spoken.

———·—·———

As I reached the group, I stepped closer to Maureen. Even in the starlit night, I could tell by her still-damp cheeks that she'd been crying. "What the hell did I miss?"

Maureen spouted, "Daniel came back."

"You look like shit. Why don't we take a break?"

We made our way to the back of the keeper's house and gathered around the picnic tables. I unclipped the radio on my belt and pressed the button. "Ron to base camp."

"Janet here. What, Ron?"

"We're gonna take a break. Why don't you grab some water and snacks and join us here?"

Halfway through the break, I looked at Maureen, who was sitting on the bench, pendulum in hand. As if she sensed me, she raised her head and said, "There's someone here. It's a woman."

I grabbed my EMF meter and walked over to her. I began waving it wildly around like a fool. "I got nothing."

Maureen spoke up, "She's gardening. Lower it. She's bent over."

I lowered the meter. As I did, the red light flashed into the night.

Jim joined me with his meter. It responded in the same manner.

Jeremy took a step forward. "Can you tell who she is?"

Maureen hesitated, then said, "I think she was the lighthouse keeper's mistress. She liked it here because people made fun of her in town." She smiled. "In fact, I can see her tending to her roses."

Jeremy asked Maureen if she could pinpoint the time period. Maureen seemed to concentrate harder but shook her head no, then spoke, "She's gone."

No sooner had the words left her lips than both our meters went dead.

As the cold, damp seacoast air coated our skin, we sat, contemplating what had just occurred. *Had we just contacted the spirit of a lighthouse keeper's mistress?*

Jeremy's voice shattered my thoughts, "Let's go in the keepers' house."

———·—

The floor creaked as we entered the house. The screen door banged behind us as Ron led our entourage down a short, narrow corridor and into a room filled with desks. It wasn't quite what I had imagined. As the rest of the group milled around chatting, I found myself curious and took the opportunity to wander about. My way of closing out the "noise," reaching out to sense any lingering energy.

"Where did Maureen go?" I heard Ron's irritated voice when he realized I wasn't there.

"Maureen, where are you?" Ron bellowed.

Without responding, I walked into the room to Ron's glare. Typical.

"You're always disappearing," he moaned. Then as if he had thought about it, he said, "Did you sense anything?"

"No, not really," I shrugged.

"All right, then let's go upstairs."

The old stairs groaned beneath our weight as we ascended to the second floor. I turned and glanced behind me, halfheartedly wondering if the stairs would collapse. Reaching the landing of the second floor, Ron led us single file down a narrow corridor to what appeared to be a very tiny kitchen area. Three of us could barely fit in the confined space. Ron stood to my right, Karen to my left, while the rest of the group were strung out along the narrow passageway. The darkness of the room was interrupted by the methodical flashing green light of the lighthouse, which penetrated the window to my right.

Karen held the recorder in an attempt to capture some EVPs, to no avail.

A sudden swoosh of energy told me we weren't alone. *"Someone is here that wants to communicate."*

"Who?" Ron asked.

A scuffling to my left caught my attention. I looked above Karen's head and could see Jeremy snaking his way through the group to join us.

I pulled my pendulum out of my pocket and connected with the eager spirit whose energy grew by the minute.

"It's a woman. A very gentle soul," I said.

Jeremy stepped in closer.

My mind raced with thoughts that were not my own. *"I feel like she passed away relatively recently. I'm getting that the lighthouse was her life, and even in death she wants to be here."*

My whole body began to tingle as the excited spirit's energy soared. In a thought, not of my own, I said, *"She wants to thank you."*

"Is it me?" Ron chimed in.

"No."

He grumbled, *"It never is."*

Jeremy, apparently intrigued, said, *"Is it me?"*

I closed my eyes for a mental confirmation and felt a spike in energy for the second time. *"I want to thank you for the gift you gave me."*

"I think I know who it might be," Jeremy added.

"Her name begins with a C. Con . . ."

"Is it Connie?" Jeremy continued.

The energy surged again. This time it didn't wane. "Yes," I replied. My voice sounded strange to my own ears. I swear I sounded like an old woman.

"Maureen, are you okay?" Because I was unable to respond, Ron continued, "Do you have anything else you want to tell us?"

My head began to swim. Connie's spirit, so excited with the possibility of breathing one last time, jumped fully in, taking over my body, inadvertently pushing me out. Seconds later, I watched from above as the weight of my body collapsed to the floor, grazing the chrome and vinyl chair that Ron attempted to slide beneath me.

"My God, is she all right?" Jeremy cried out.

As I lay there, slowly regaining my consciousness, fragments of the ensuing chaos began to take hold. From a distance, I heard Ron's voice. "Anybody have any water?"

Moments later, I felt Ron's and Jeremy's arms attempt to lift me off the floor and onto the nearby chair. Still groggy, I found it difficult to help them.

"Maureen, are you okay?" Ron asked in a concerned voice.

"Yeah, I'm okay. Just give me a second," I lied.

"You look a little pale. Why don't you rest a minute?" Ron turned to the group trying to crowd into the small room. "Come on, let's give her some air."

"I'll stay with her," Roxie said as she bellied her way through the crowd.

With the last of his words, Ron and the remainder of the team descended the stairs.

"Maureen, are you sure you're feeling okay? I can get you some more water."

As Roxie spoke, an image of a bouquet of flowers popped into my head. "Roxie, I think Connie has something else to say."

"She does?" Her voice wavered.

"Yes. She wants to thank you for the flowers with large pink buds."

Taken aback, with tears in her eyes, she responded, "Oh, my God, you're not going to believe this." She hesitated. "Connie Small was the last lighthouse keeper's wife. She died in February. I wanted to do something special for her, so I picked up some pink tulips and brought them with me to her funeral. After the services, me and Ken waited to be the last one to step up to Connie's coffin. As tears ran down my cheeks, the minister came up to me and told me I could place the flowers inside the coffin." Her lips tugged up in a sad smile, "Maureen, no one knew that I had brought her the flowers, let alone put them with her, except me, my husband, and the minister. And here it is, six months later and you're telling me she wants to thank me for the flowers. That's unbelievable!"

I stood up and gave Roxie a big hug.

Since it was nearly three a.m., we began to pack up our equipment and call it a night. We removed the equipment from the base of the lighthouse and headed to our cars. As I gazed at the starlit night, a chill came over me. Across the wave-crested water, a sudden fog bank began to roll in. "Hey, guys. Look."

Silence fell upon the group as the swirling mist, lit by the green light of the lighthouse, encompassed us.

I stood in awe at the sudden change in the atmosphere. Ron spoke up, "Cool. Let's go up to the tower."

Jeremy unlocked the door. Collectively, we scurried up the winding stairs to the lamp room. One by one, we squeezed ourselves through the tiny door leading out to the deck, which was slick beneath our feet from the moisture in the air.

Standing in the open air, arms stretched wide, I felt this was the spirits' way of saying good-bye and thanking us. Within moments, the surreal experience dissipated. Before we knew it, it was gone. Just like that. It's moments like this that make what we do worthwhile.

OUR THOUGHTS

MAUREEN:

This particular investigation was intriguing to me for many reasons: first and foremost, when I channeled Connie. When you're communicating with the dead, it's very rare to happen upon a spirit that existed in the same century as yourself (aside from reading for clients, that is). Connie Small, the last lighthouse keeper's wife, was one of those special spirits. Several months later, when we were invited to present the findings of our investigation at a special presentation, I was blown away by seeing the life-size projected image of Connie on the screen. In fact, I was so overwhelmed with emotion, when I saw her face on the screen, that it was all I could do to control the onslaught of tears. It isn't every day that I am given this rare opportunity to come face to face with someone I've just recently, spiritually, communed with.

RON:

This investigation produced a potpourri of evidence: there was the reputable testimony of Coast Guard personnel; a great EVP by Karen where she picked up the nickname of the longest-serving lighthouse keeper; Dan capturing another great image with his thermal imager; and Maureen's amazing impressions of the spirits— especially that of Daniel and his death in the explosion at the fort. What had to impress everyone, including Roxie and Jeremy, was the channeling of Connie Small. She revealed that Roxie had put a bouquet of big pink flowers in her coffin. This event occurred months before Maureen even met Roxie and was information that only Roxie, her husband, and the preacher knew.

Daniel Lady Farm

Case File: 1905622 Gettysburg

Location: Gettysburg, Pennsylvania

History: The historic Daniel Lady Farm served as Major General Edward Johnson's base camp for the Confederate attack on Cult's Hill. It also served as a Confederate field hospital during the battle.

Reported Paranormal Activity: Phantom odors, ghostly apparitions, temperature changes, and malfunctioning electronics.

Clients: Mark (author) and Carol Nesbitt (wife), Laine Crosby (medium).

Investigators: Ron (lead investigator), Maureen (trance medium), Jim (photographer), St. Jan (Ron's wife).

Press: N/A.

Purpose of Investigation: While attending the Ghost of Gettysburg conference, Mark Nesbitt and company asked us to investigate the farm to provide them with our impressions.

I rapped my knuckles against the metal door adjoining our two rooms—Maureen and her husband in one, Jan and I in the other.

The metal door swayed open. Maureen stood there looking tired from the long trip. "You look like shit, Kid," I said.

"Thanks, Ron. You always know the right words to say. It's been a long trip."

"I want to go downstairs and check out the venue. Do you want to go?"

"Nah. I think I'll take a nap instead."

"Where's Steve?"

"He's downstairs. Probably at the bar with Jim."

As I looked past Maureen and into the room, movement to my left caught my attention. I turned quickly to see a dark shadow leave her bathroom and exit her room through the hall door. The lock clicked and the do not disturb sign swayed back and forth.

"Did I just see what I think I saw?" Maureen asked.

"What the hell?" I said as I bolted for the door. I opened it quickly and looked down the long corridor.

No one was there.

I stepped back inside, shut the door, and turned to face Maureen, who was standing there, mouth agape. "There was no one there, Maureen. I swear." I replayed the event in my mind's eye. "What the heck just happened?"

"I don't know. I just saw the same thing you did. A black shadow going out the door."

"Looks like this is going to be a good weekend." I grinned at Maureen. "Still want to take your nap?"

"Ah, yeah. I think so," Maureen said, even though her words didn't match her expression.

"All right, I'm going downstairs. I'll see you in about an hour."

———·———

With Ron gone and the room finally quiet, I lay atop the covers of the bed and closed my eyes. Exhaustion set in. My eyes grew heavy. My consciousness began to wane.

On the brink of sleep, my third eye began to pulse.

I was no longer alone.

I slowly forced my eyes open as I felt the gentle touch of an astral hand anointing my forehead.

Unable to move, my eyes began to focus on the figure hunched over me. Although I couldn't see his face, I could clearly see the brown woolen cloak he wore. Beads and rope belt. Although this situation might be terrifying to most people, I could sense a calmness in his energy. I knew I had nothing to fear.

As quickly as he appeared, he disappeared.

Once again as before, I heard the sound of a knock on the door between our room and Ron's. Sitting up, I rose from the bed, ran my hand over my shirt to remove the wrinkles, and scurried to door to open it.

As if looking for the shadow from earlier, Ron peeked his head into the room. He paused for a minute. "You ready, Kid?"

"Ron, you're not going to believe this, but I think I was just blessed by a monk."

"What do you mean you were just blessed by a monk?"

"I'm telling you. I was lying in bed, just about to fall asleep, and I opened my eyes to see a monk blessing me."

"Get out of here! Seriously?"

"As serious as a heart attack." I couldn't help but wonder what it was that we would encounter this weekend that I needed the blessing of a monk.

"Wow, this weekend keeps getting better and better. I can't wait until we get to do the investigation."

I could feel the gravel through the soles of my sneakers as I stood in the driveway between Jan and Maureen, listening to Mark Nesbitt at the Daniel Lady Farm.

Mark, projecting his voice for the group of us, said, "We are on the extreme left flank of the Confederate lines here at

Gettysburg. The barn and the farmhouse became Confederate General Johnson's division hospital. They were filled with the wounded and dying soldiers." He paused, pointed to the barn, and continued his discourse. "Outside the windows over there were pyramids of amputated arms, legs, hands, and feet. These were the result of the mini balls, which were 58-caliber soft-lead ammo. The name *mini* comes from the guy who invented it, and not the size of the ball, as many believe."

"Pyramids of limbs, that's gross," I said.

"Yes, they could do an amputation in two to three minutes. The soldier's suffering was over, and they could attempt to recover. Recovery was difficult because they knew little about antiseptics. This was before the work of Pasteur and Lister. The poor soldiers would have dirty rags put on their wounds, and they might be fine for a week or two. Then gangrene and tetanus would set in, and then they would die."

While Mark finished his speech, I glanced at Mark's wife and noticed she was holding a pair of dowsing rods (L-rods). Waiting for the right moment, I spoke up, "I see, Carol, you have dowsing rods with you. What are you going to do with them?"

"When we work with Laine, our resident psychic, I usually bring them so if she asks a question, I will have her repeat it and verify her answer with the dowsing rods."

DOWSING ROD (L-ROD)

Similar to a pendulum, an L-shaped metal rod that is used for dowsing.

"Do you ever use one of these, an EMF meter?" I said, waving it before her. "Oh, crap. Speaking of EMF meters, looks like my batteries are dead."

"No, we haven't used them, and the one nice thing about the dowsing roads is that they have no batteries. You know, Ron, that if you go into a haunted location, the spirit can drain the batteries from your meters, cameras, and recorders, but not from the dowsing rods. There is an advantage to simple equipment."

"Want to hear something funny? We had a ghost-hunting seminar last month, and during the event, this girl by the name of Stacey Caira took me aside and told me something that nobody ever thought about."

"What?"

"She told me she wore a hearing aid, and every time she went to one of our events, her hearing aid batteries went dead. She finally gave up on wearing them at our events."

"Wow, I never thought of that. Maybe Mark and I should start checking for pacemakers on our tours. That could be a problem."

The group chuckled.

Maureen joined in. "I'm a dowser too, but for ease of use, the pendulum's my favorite. In fact, I taught Ron."

"Yeah. And you charged me for it, too. Maureen's also a trance channeler."

Laine, who had been quiet to this point, spoke up, "So spirits come into your body?"

Maureen nodded.

Laine continued, "Okay, I don't do that. That's absolutely amazing."

"I don't do it all the time. Only when the moment feels right. Sometimes when I open myself up to communicate, I do get an aggressive spirit that doesn't respect the Karmic laws and jumps right in."

"That doesn't sound pleasant to me."

"It's not."

"Sorry to interrupt," Mark said, "but why don't you follow me over to the barn."

Standing on the dirt floor, in the center of the barn, my eyes darted to and fro. I could feel the history in the atmosphere.

Mark walked over to the far wall and began, "This is the original barn, and if you look over here, you can see where some Confederate soldiers carved their initials and regiments right in this board." Mark pointed to the far corner. "If you look over there, see how that part of the wall is different?"

"Yeah," Jan said.

"That's because a shell exploded just outside of the wall." Mark pointed up. "Take a look up there. Can you see that piece of metal in the beam? That's a piece of the shell that exploded."

"Wow. That's amazing," Maureen said.

Mark waved his hand out before him. "Can you imagine this floor covered with twenty to twenty-five years of manure and then in come all these wounded soldiers with open wounds lying in here on the ground because they didn't know any better. That is why so many of them died afterwards."

Maureen spoke up, "I'm sensing that they would do the operations on tables here and then move them off to the side of the barn afterwards."

Mark replied, "That's fairly accurate. A lot of the time they would use a makeshift operating table. They would just take a door off the hinge and place it on a couple of sawhorses, where they would saw off the limbs."

"Sawhorses, is that a pun?" I joked.

"Ha-ha. No." Mark laughed.

"Hey, Ron," Maureen said as she stood by the wall with the names carved into the wooden planks. "I keep hearing, 'Don't forget me.'"

Jan responded, "Oh, don't worry. You won't be forgotten."

Tears began to roll down Maureen's cheeks.

"Pretty heavy, huh?" Laine said as she approached Maureen. "Come on. Let's get some air," she said as she placed her arm on Maureen's shoulder to comfort her and gingerly guided her outside.

"We might as well go, too," I said.

I walked up to Maureen and Laine. "Yeah, so that was a good idea, huh?"

Maureen looked up at me from behind a tissue. "Yeah, and we haven't even toured the house."

"Are you all right?" I asked.

Maureen sniffled and said, "Yeah, I'm fine."

"Your nose looks cute red," I quipped, trying to lighten the moment.

"Ha-ha, Ron."

Mark led us around to the other side of the barn. Standing in front of the door to the second floor, he said, "Look here. You can drive a wagon right into the second floor. This is what they call a Pennsylvania bank barn. Over there is where they believe they piled up the bodies."

"You know, Mark, as I'm standing here, I'm hearing loud booms and muffled noises," Maureen said.

"Where? What direction?" Mark asked, his voice filled with excitement.

Maureen raised her arm and pointed to a high ridge. "Over there."

"Funny you say that because there was a huge artillery battery over there between the Confederate batteries on the ridge and the Union artillery on Cemetery Hill. This is what you're probably hearing." Mark continued, "Are you getting any names?"

"No. Not right now. There are just too many of them."

I had an idea. "Maureen, do you want to try your pendulum?"

"You try it. I don't have mine with me. Do you have yours?"

"Of course, I do. Remember, I'm your pocketbook."

After a couple of minutes of dowsing, Mark spoke up, "So many psychics who come here are just so overwhelmed."

"I can totally understand why." A sad smile crossed Maureen's lips. "Wait. I'm picking up a name. It begins with a D. Dave." She gasped. "My God, there are so many here. I get the sense that they know who we are and are glad we're here so they won't be forgotten."

Carol said, "We had a friend here who was a psychic. It was just a little while ago. She told Mark that they were always so glad to see him, because he always brings people by who can hear them."

"My heart is breaking. My God, they were so young. So many spirits." Maureen's eyes brimmed with tears.

"Yes. It's a bit overwhelming. Fifty-one thousand casualties. That's an entire football stadium. It's totally inconceivable," Mark replied. Then he continued, "Even those who survived the battle would come back for reunions and whatnot. If it meant so much to them when they were alive, then what makes you think that they wouldn't return when they died."

Jan spoke up, "It was such a seminal part of their lives, they certainly wouldn't forget it."

"Absolutely," Mark agreed.

I had a sudden thought, "On that note, Mark, let me ask you this. You have been here a long time. Do you notice if there is more activity on the anniversary of the battle than other times?"

"That's a good question, Ron. Well, there are a lot more people here during the anniversary, so therefore, a lot more people to witness the paranormal activity. At other times, the activity may still be occurring, but there is no one there to witness it. So, it's kind of like a catch-22." He paused, then said, "Do you want to go over to the house now?"

I glanced at Maureen. As if she were reading my mind, she said, "We can go. I'm all right now. As an FYI, Ron, I will tell you, as you and Mark were speaking, I could sense a man here trying to talk to me, but I couldn't hear him because he doesn't have a voice box."

Laine chimed in, "I could see a man standing to the right of you, Maureen, trying to tell you something."

"Yes, there was something wrong with his throat, like it was slit."

"I'm just curious, Laine. Are there any female spirits here?" I asked.

"Yes, there is. The owner of the house. What's her name, Carol?"

"Rebecca."

"Yes, that's it, Rebecca. Even in death she was quite a funny lady. One time, we had a psychic here who said she liked to entertain in the front room. Rebecca spoke to me and said, 'That's not true. I would have my friends sit at the kitchen table.' Then she told me that when she came back into the house after the soldiers left, she had to do a lot of scrubbing."

"Yeah, I bet she's still scrubbing," I said.

Mark chuckled. "That's probably true," he said as he unlocked the back door to the house.

No sooner had we walked into the kitchen than Maureen grimaced. "Ewe. It smells like burning flesh in here."

"Burning flesh?" Mark asked. "For a minute I was wondering why you would have said that, until I remembered that they burned the limbs. So, that is what you were probably smelling."

Grabbing her arm, Maureen said, "I'm beginning to feel the energy really strong, and I got to tell you that my arm is killing me."

"Did Ron tell me that you channel?" Mark's voice wavered as he asked.

"Yes," Maureen said.

Sensing Mark's reluctance, I asked, "Do you want her to channel?"

His voice trembled as he said, "No, not really. It really scares me."

Maureen interjected. "I'm picking up on someone right now who wants to come through, but I don't want him to."

"Why? Is he bad?" I asked.

"No, I don't think so. He's standing next to me, and my arm is killing me. He had his limb cut off, and he's trying to tell me he's not dead. It's frustrating him. He doesn't understand why nobody can see him."

Maureen let out a deep groan and stumbled back against the kitchen counter.

Hearing the commotion, Laine rushed into the kitchen. "Is she channeling now?"

"Yes."

Laine took a step toward Maureen and addressed the spirit within her, "Can you tell me your name?" She then said, "I think it's the guy I was talking to in the kitchen. I think his name is Johnson."

The spirit within Maureen replied in a deep, loud voice, "It's S-l-a-t-e-r."

Laine stepped back, "What is your name?"

Once again, in voice not her own, Maureen bellowed, "S-l-a-t-e-r."

"Thank you," Laine replied timidly.

Realizing I needed to take control of the situation, I began to question the spirit within. "Slater, what's your rank? Do you have something you want to tell us?"

No reply. Maureen shifted her weight, visibly agitated.

In an attempt to comfort the spirit, I said, "It's okay, Slater, it's okay."

The hardened stare of a moment ago was now gone. Maureen was back.

She began coughing.

"Are you all right, Kid?"

Rubbing her arm, she replied, "Oooh, my arm is killing me."

As if feeling bad for Maureen, Laine interjected, "This is not a nice place. There's a lot of pain here."

"I feel like I'm going to be sick. I smell all kinds of horrible smells. Blood. Urine. Feces. And there's another smell, something I'm not familiar with." Maureen suddenly stopped speaking and began to waver. "Everything is going white right now. Fading out. I can't see anything."

I grabbed Maureen's arm. "Do you want to step outside for a few minutes? It's a little lighter out there."

"No. Give me a minute."

"White light. White light. Are you okay?" I said, once again, trying to lighten the moment.

Maureen doubled over. "I just want to be sick. I feel body parts and blood and pain. It's torture. It's awful. People being held down, and other people doing all kinds of horrible things to them. I'm hearing all these voices at once. Yelling and screaming in my ear."

Not giving her a choice, I said, "Let's get you out of here. Come on."

In the hall, as we were heading out to the front door, Mark approached us, "Hey, Ron, look. My camera just turned on by itself."

Maureen moaned and then threw her hand out against the door jam. "Ron, I've got to go in here."

"I don't think that's a good idea."

"You don't understand. I have to go."

Before I could stop her, she had already entered the room. She began screaming. Her body trembled as she doubled over at the waist. As if fighting an unseen enemy, she thrashed her arms about. "No! No! You can't do this!"

Still struggling, she screamed louder.

Laine screeched, "Ron, you have to get her out of here!"

"Maureen, come on. Let's go." I reached out to grab her, and she whacked my hand away.

Still fighting my efforts, she threw herself back against the wall.

She sobbed, slid down the wall, and sat on the floor.

Placing my hands on her shoulders, I said, "Maureen, if you don't come with me, I'm going to throw you over my shoulder and carry you out of here."

As if regaining control, Maureen began to cough. I helped her up to her feet and guided her down the hallway and out of the house. The trembling that was once prevalent before had now subsided. "Are you feeling better?"

It took a moment for her to respond. She took a deep breath and said, "I'm a little weak but fine."

"Hey, I bet it builds an appetite?" I chuckled. *Jeez*, I thought to myself, *how many times tonight am I going to have to try to lighten the moment?*

The screen door opened and Mark poked his head out.

"Sorry, Mark. Can you give us five more minutes?"

"Sure," he said as the door closed behind him.

I called out for Jan, who joined us momentarily. "Will you stay with Maureen?"

"Sure, I'd be glad to," she said as I walked back in the house to meet Mark.

"Is Maureen all right?" Mark asked.

"Yes, she'll be fine. She does this all the time."

"We have had so many people come in here and completely lose it. Let me show you something," he said, ushering me back into the room that had caused so much distress to Maureen.

Standing in the center of the room, he said, "This is where they would have had the operating table. Over there, where Maureen was, you can see the blood stains on the floor. If you look real close, you can see a handprint. See. Four fingers and a thumb," he said, tracing the outline with his finger atop the hardwood floor. "This is probably where some poor guy was sitting waiting his turn dripping blood. I can only imagine that when he got called, he pushed himself up off the floor with this hand."

"Wow! That's unbelievable."

"It is. And after all these years, you can still see the bloodstains in these floorboards. And if you think that is unbelievable," he paused, "the weirdest story that ever happened to me happened here. One day I got a call from the caretaker and he said, 'Mark, if you want to see a paranormal event happening right before your eyes, hurry up and come out here.' So I grabbed my equipment and got here as quick as possible. When I arrived, I wasn't sure what to expect. Was something going to fly out the door at me? I had no idea. I was greeted by the caretaker and followed him into this room. It was about 12:30 in the afternoon. I'm standing here, and I'm looking all around and right in front of the fireplace was this," he said as he grabbed an eight-by-twelve photo off the table.

I took the photo out of Mark's hand for a closer look. "Oh, my God!"

Mark pointed to the photograph, "See the liquid on the floor. Look, can you see how it was running? See right here, the drops. They were red. Rust colored. Still damp. I looked up at the ceiling to see if anything had dripped. There was no sign of anything. So, I got a piece of Kleenex and dipped the tissue in the liquid and took a sample."

"Really?"

"Yeah. I spent about a half hour out here and took lots and lots of photos and footage of it and then I left. But get this:

about three hours later, I received another call from the care-taker. 'Mark, come back out here. It's gone.' I said, 'You're kidding,' before jumping in the car and driving back. When I came into this room, it looked like it does now," he said while pointing to the floor. "In fact, this is cleaner than it was then. Because when I walked in that day, there was just a very tiny, thin layer of dust on the floor. As if the liquid was never there. So, I ran out to my car to check on the sample. It was still there. So later that week, I sent the Kleenex out to a very prestigious forensic laboratory for analysis. When the results came back, the analysis was that it was human blood."

"Really? That's amazing. So actual, physical evidence? That's totally awesome."

"Standing here, we can see we have 140-year-old bloodstains that poor Rebecca scrubbed and scrubbed with lye soap for twenty years and couldn't get them out. Yet these," he said, pointing back to the picture, "disappeared in a couple of hours. Like they were never there."

"Mark, I have never, never heard of a case like this in my life. That is so totally awesome." I reiterated, "I think it's phenomenal. Absolutely phenomenal."

"What still amazes me to this day is that, although the whole farm is drenched in history, every single sensitive who visits here becomes focused on just one afternoon and one evening, in July 1863."

OUR THOUGHTS

MAUREEN:

The catastrophic events that transpired in July 1863, the loss of so many souls in such a short amount of time, have left a haunting imprint in Gettysburg—one that I believe can be felt by even the most desensitized person. For those of us who are sensitive to energies, it can be particularly grueling to endure. While I have visited Gettysburg on several occasions, memories of the Daniel Lady Farm are among those that will not easily be forgotten. Why? Well, let's just say that it's difficult to erase the memory of not only seeing through a spirit's eyes, but reliving the horror of the moment, as he waited in line to have his limb cut off.

RON:

This investigation gave us a unique opportunity to delve into an amazing site drenched in history, blood, and especially for Maureen, pain. Mark Nesbitt's knowledge of the history, coupled with Maureen's impressions, gave me a whole new perspective of the location that touched my soul. Our experiences with the phantom visitor in the hotel also told me that sometimes there is no escape from the paranormal, no matter where you are.

Sleeping with the Dead

Case File: 283498 Converted condos

Location: Dracut, Massachusetts

History: House built circa 1893, now divided into three condominiums.

Reported Paranormal Activity: Apparitions, poltergeist activity.

Clients: Ron (condo owner) and his girlfriend.

Investigators: Ron (lead investigator), Maureen (trance medium), Karen (EVP specialist), Jim (photographer).

Press: N/A.

Purpose of Investigation: To try to explain the strange occurrences at the owner's home.

I arrived in my office and threw my briefcase on the desk and immediately noticed the red flashing light on the answering machine. I hit the button and listened.

"Hi, Ron. This is Joe. We met at church. Can you give me a call when you have a minute?"

Joe is the curator of a local historical society, whose headquarters we've investigated before. Although I had a ton of things to do, I grabbed the receiver and dialed.

After a short conversation, Joe told me he had been contacted by a guy in Dracut who was looking for information on the history of his property. During their conversation, he had told Joe that he believed that his property was haunted. Joe informed him about the New England Ghost Project and what we do. And now he wanted an investigation. I told Joe we would be happy to oblige.

———————

As we turned onto Pineland Avenue, I couldn't believe it had been two weeks since I had last spoken to the homeowner. Time seemed to drag. Within a matter of minutes, we were at our destination. Now at the location, I took a moment to assess the old house before us. The white, weathered clapboard siding had seen better days. I found it hard to imagine that this once-landmark home was now divided into three condos.

We removed our equipment from the trunk and slammed the lid. Climbing the uneven stone stairs, I reached out and grabbed the twisted wrought-iron railing to steady myself. Before we could even ring the bell, our presence was announced by a loud bark. *Great, a dog! Something else to annoy me.*

The deadbolt clicked just before the solid wood door swung open. The hall light projected the silhouette of an average height, slightly heavy figure of a man standing in the doorway.

"Hi, I'm Ron," the man spoke in soft voice.

"So am I," I replied with a chuckle. I reached out and shook his hand. "I'm Ron from the New England Ghost Project."

"Great. I've been expecting you. Come on in." He backed up and ushered us into the hallway. "I'm eager to have you and your team investigate. These last two weeks seemed to take forever. . . ."

We followed him into a small living room to the right of the stairs. And before we had a chance to sit, he began to tell us his story.

"Strange things began happening when I started doing renovations. The hall light would turn off and on, and objects seemed to move by themselves. My girlfriend, a devout Catholic from Colombia, and who senses things, said that there's 'woowoo' here."

I thought to myself, *What the hell is 'woowoo'?*

His demeanor suddenly changed as if reliving the moment. His eyes became transfixed on the stairs in the adjacent hall. "Each night at about eleven p.m., a dark shadow appears. It traverses the stairs to the second floor." He raised his voice. "I see it as clear as you are to me." Looking at the dog sitting quietly by his legs, he said, "Even my dog barks at it."

He gazed at each of us in an obvious attempt to gauge our reaction. Satisfied, he continued. Eyes wide, voice trembling, he said, "I know you're not going to believe this, but I promise you I'm not lying." Like taking an oath at a court trial, he raised his hand in front of us. "This is the truth, so help me God."

"We're not here to judge," I said. "Continue. We're listening."

"Well, sometimes at night, when I'm lying in bed, I feel the presence of someone or something climbing into bed with me." He shivered. "Almost immediately, that side of my body feels frigidly cold. I lie there, seemingly for hours, praying it goes away. But it never does. Finally, when I'm able to speak, I beg *it* to please leave me alone. And slowly the coldness dissipates." He turned back to us, "I thought I was going crazy, until I brought up the subject with the condo association. The other two owners reported that they all had experienced similar incidences."

Karen, who was enamored by every word, replied, "Oh, that *is* disturbing."

"Are those the stairs where you see the shadow?" I said, pointing into the hall.

"Yes. Come with me. I'll show you what I'm talking about."
No sooner had we entered the hallway than Maureen suddenly
stopped in her tracks.

---

*As soon as I entered the hall, I felt a presence. Ron's EMF blared,
confirming my thoughts that something was with us. Without
waiting for Ron to ask and not wanting to lose the opportunity, I
retrieved my pendulum and began dowsing.*

*Feeling it was a feminine energy, I asked, "Is this a woman?" The
weight of the stone suddenly grew heavy, as it began to rotate counterclockwise, confirming what I already knew.*

*As the pendulum spun through a series of questions, it revealed
she was seventy-five years old, Irish, married with five children, and
worked in the mills. And although the homeowner's story of just a
moment ago was unnerving to say the least, I felt the warmth of her
presence. To me, I sensed she was kind and loving. Certainly, not
someone to fear.*

*I glanced to the homeowner who stood by the hall mirror. "I really
feel she's attracted to you. She doesn't want to leave. You remind her
of her husband."*

*"What?!" He grimaced. "That's creepy. I guess my girlfriend was
right." He reiterated, "There is 'woowoo' here."*

*"I really don't think it's as creepy as you think. I believe she's just
reliving her life. Each night she goes through the routine of walking
upstairs and going to bed. It just happens that your bed is in her old
room." Just then, I felt the tickle of air as a voice whispered in my
ear. "She just told me her name is Lillian."*

*Suddenly, feeling the energy wane, I pulled the moldavite out of
my pocket. Like a tuner on a radio, it helps me focus and tune in to
the spirit more easily.*

"Maureen, can you ask her how she died?" Ron spoke up.

MOLDAVITE

A medium to dark green stone (tektite) named after the Moldau River in what is now the Czech Republic. Its formation coincided with the crash of a large meteorite in the Bohemian plateau. Spiritual properties include transformation, connection to higher vibrations, cleansing, protection, and increased incidence of synchronistic experiences.

"I can ask." I clasped my fingers around the stone. Feeling the vibration increase, I said, "Lillian, can you tell us how you died?" Words I would quickly come to regret.

I felt a sudden tightness in my chest. My breathing became labored as if my lungs were filling with water. I began to cough. The sound raspy, wet to my own ears. My coughing intensified. My lungs burned as I gasped for air. As if the spirit realized the effect she had on me, she withdrew.

Slowly, the pain in my chest dissipated. My throat was still raw as I struggled to catch my breath.

Ron, realizing what I needed, grabbed hold of my arm and guided me to a nearby chair.

Between shallow breaths, I blurted out, "I think she died of consumption."

He glared at me. "No shit. I thought you were going to, too."

I didn't want to admit it, but I was a little nervous, too. Being empathic, once again, I should have known better to phrase my questions a little differently. Reliving someone else's death is no picnic. I still remember my experience at the Lizzie Borden House.

As I sat regaining my strength, Karen addressed the homeowner, "Ron, do you have a son?"

"Yes, I do. His name is Matthew."

"For some reason I'm drawn to the photograph in the living room of the little boy. I think maybe she likes him when he visits," Karen said.

"That's comforting."

Feeling better, I rose to my feet. *"Ron, if you're ready, I am."*

"I'm as ready as a heart attack."

We climbed the stairs. As we walked in and out of the various rooms on the second floor, I felt little. I stopped to reach out to see if Lillian, who had been so prevalent earlier, was still with us. But there was no response.

Sensing nothing, I knew she was gone. *"Ron, I can't sense her or anyone else anymore."*

With that, we headed back downstairs to the living room.

As we discussed what we experienced, Karen thumbed through her recordings. She had been recording on and off all night long. Something must have caught her ear because she interrupted our conversation. With a hint of excitement in her voice, she said, *"Didn't you say your son's name is Matthew?"*

"Yes."

"Listen to this!" Karen pressed the button.

Through the static of the recorder, we could hear Karen's voice as she asked, *"Ron, do you have a son?"* Before he could even respond, we could clearly hear the voice of a woman with an Irish accent reply in a whisper, *"Matthew."*

A collective gasp filled the room.

"Can you play that again?" the homeowner asked.

Karen eagerly obliged by playing it several times.

By the fifth time or so, my head felt as if it was going to explode. The night had taken its toll, and I was pleased when Ron spoke up, *"I think it's time to wrap it up."*

We gathered our equipment, and before we headed out, Ron asked the homeowner, *"Do you have any questions for us?"*

"No, not now." He reached out and shook Ron's hand. "I really want to thank you guys for coming here tonight. It was amazing. You answered a lot of my questions. I feel a lot better now." His lips tugged up in a smile. "I can't wait to tell my girlfriend and the other condo owners all about it. Once again, thank you very much."

Over the sound of the tires thumping over the uneven pavement, Ron asked, "What the hell is it with that stone you used. Are you crazy? You could have killed yourself."

I chuckled in response. "It wasn't the stone. It was how I phrased the question."

"Well, don't do that again," he grunted.

Awe, the curmudgeon has a heart.

OUR THOUGHTS

MAUREEN:

Even with all the spirits I'd communicated with over the years, the thought of a spirit climbing into bed with someone each night was creepy, even to me—that is, until I felt the energy of the spirit and realized that to her, it was a normal act, a memory. As far as she was concerned, she was just climbing into bed. This situation made me realize the similarities between the living and dead, and how sometimes, all it takes is some understanding and to have the objectivity to step back and take a look at a situation through another person's eyes.

RON:

This was a short investigation with little hard evidence, but it taught me how real paranormal experiences can affect some people's lives. It still left me wondering what the hell "woowoo" is.

Ghost Bride

Case File: 1905324 The Ghost Bride

Location: Cape Elizabeth, Maine

History: Inn by the Sea was built in 1986, replacing the former Crescent Beach Inn. It sits just above Crescent Beach and is adjacent to a small cemetery that contains the grave of Lydia Carver, a bride-to-be who perished in an 1807 storm.

Reported Paranormal Activity: Apparitions of ghostly bride, objects that move by themselves, and disembodied voices.

Clients: Roxie Zwicker (event host).

Investigators: Ron (lead investigator), Maureen (trance medium), Jim (photographer), St. Jan (Ron's wife), Stephen (Maureen's husband).

Press: N/A.

Purpose of Investigation: Dinner event.

Sitting in my suite at the Inn by the Sea, I glanced down at my watch. Where the hell is she? Here I am ready to do a remote live broadcast for WCCM and once again, I'm by myself.

"Ten seconds to air."

Without skipping a beat, I jumped into the opening. "Good evening, everyone. Welcome to another broadcast of *Ghost*

Chronicles on WCCM. I am Ron Kolek, your host, the gate-keeper to the realm of the unknown, the unexplained, and the unbelievable. New England's own Van Helsing. And with me is my cohost . . . well, she is not actually with me. My cohost, who is in her car, somewhere. Where are you?"

Over the air, the sound of Maureen's voice crackled through her phone. "Right now, I am on 495."

"Okay, so . . . correction, the Queen of Pain is with me. Out there, somewhere."

"Hi, everybody."

"So, here we are for a big dinner event in Cape Elizabeth, Maine, and we are going on a quest to find the ghost bride, Lydia Carver."

"That's right. But I don't know about your idea of trying to marry her off." Maureen chuckled.

"I think it is a great idea. She's been here for almost two hundred years, and if you can 'trance-medium' her and I give her the vows and marry her off, she can go on to the happy hunting grounds or the light or wherever that is."

"'Trance-medium' her? So you want me to channel her and you will marry her off?"

"There you go."

"I don't know about that."

"I brought a wedding dress."

"Oh, you are so kind," Maureen said, her voice dripping with sarcasm.

"Hey, I just thought of this. We're going to go outside, in Maine, in February, in the cold. Right?"

"Yes."

"How will we know when there is a cold spot?"

The sound of laughter burst through the phone. "Yes, that might be a little difficult to do. For me, it will be more about locating the energy and not focusing on a cold spot, but you on the other hand might have a problem."

"So this will be kind of new for us because we have never done an investigation in the *dead* of the winter."

"Ha-ha, no pun intended." Maureen paused. "Oh, my phone's beeping."

"They get EVPs on phones, you know. It might be Lydia calling you from the great beyond, telling you, you must get married."

"I don't think it's her. I'm already married. By the way, once is enough. And I'm really not sure what my husband would think of it anyways."

"All right, I will talk with you when you get here. See you then."

"Okay. I'm about a half hour out. See you soon." The line went dead.

I turned to my right and gave a slight nod to the slender woman sitting next to me—her indication that our interview was about to begin. I could tell by the blush rising in her cheeks that she was a bit nervous to sit next to the great Van Helsing. Through my uncontrollable smile, I spoke, "Joining us now is someone who knows a lot about the Inn by the Sea, Regina Kay."

"Hi, glad to be here with you."

"This place is actually gorgeous."

"Thank you. It's a wonderful property. We are located on Cape Elizabeth just 150 yards from Crescent Beach, where our resident ghost Lydia drowned just off that beach two hundred years ago." She paused for emphasis. "The current inn has been here for twenty years, but there has always been an inn here since 1930. It has changed hands several times."

"So it went inn and out?" *I kill myself.*

"That's right. This inn has lots of history around it, including the lovely Lydia, who has always stayed on this property."

"When did you realize she was here?"

"I have been here only for a short period of time, but there have been many stories about her that appeared in the press throughout the years. The story of Lydia Carver began in 1807. The schooner, *Charles*, was heading home to Portland from a day trip to Boston. On board were twenty-two passengers, including Captain Jacob Adam's wife. Anyone who knows the lore of the sea knows it's considered bad luck for a captain's wife to sail with him."

"I can understand that. I even hate driving with my wife."

Laughter escaped her lips. She continued, "Anyway, also on board the *Charles* was the twenty-three-year-old Lydia Carver, the soon-to-be-married daughter of a popular Freeport banker. She and some of her wedding party had gone to Boston to purchase a wedding dress and trousseau.

"The ship's journey was relatively uneventful until the *Charles* reached Casco Bay around midnight. That's when an unexpected fog bank rolled in, shrouding the shoals of Maine's rocky coast. As the fog thickened, the coastline disappeared and the schooner struck Watt's Ledge. Despite the best efforts of the crew, the *Charles* went down. All but six of the passengers perished in the shipwreck. Amongst the dead was the young bride-to-be, Lydia Carver. Her body was found the next morning washed up on Crescent Beach. Next to her was her never-worn wedding dress and trunk containing her trousseau.

"Her body was buried in the small cemetery beside the inn. Next to the cemetery is a large green lawn. In the summer, we put up tents and have weddings there. We like to believe that Lydia enjoys attending all the weddings because she never had one of her own."

"Don't you think it is sad because she was deprived of the only thing she really wanted in her life?" I interjected.

"No, I like to think of her as a friendly spirit. A happy spirit. Someone who enjoys going to the weddings, kicking up her heels, and seeing the brides and the ceremonies, because she never had one of her own. Obviously, it is a melancholy story, but I think she likes us here, and we love her."

I pointed to the gown hanging on the coat hook against the back wall. "We actually brought a wedding dress with us tonight to see if we could stir up some activity with it.

"The gown is something we call a trigger device. For instance, if a place were haunted by a child, we might bring a toy to see if the spirit would interact with it. And I'm hoping to get some interaction from Lydia."

With little emotion, Regina retorted, "It is a lovely gown. I wish you the best of luck with it."

Before I knew it, the show was over. And lo and behold, the queen made an appearance.

"Hi, Ron," Maureen said as she poked her head through the open door.

"Perfect timing. The show's all over."

"Sorry, work traffic."

"Yadda, yadda, ya."

"Whatever." Maureen, unfazed by my comment, continued, "Jan and Roxie are waiting for us to join them for dinner."

"Hang on. I need to get my equipment."

I unzipped the side pocket of my red duffle bag and removed my digital recorder and laser thermometer and placed them on the bed. I opened the end pocket where I kept my EMF meter and reached inside. It was empty. "What the hell?!"

"What's the matter, Ron?"

"I know I packed everything in my bag before I left, but my EMF meter isn't in it," I said as I continued to rifle through the bag for the third time. "That's crazy. . . ."

"Here, let me look." Maureen slid the duffle bag in front of her and removed the remaining items from the bag. Camera, cables, spare batteries, and gadgets galore. But no EMF meter. She looked up at me, her face scrunched up. "I don't know, Ron. Are you sure you packed it?"

"Course I am."

"Never mind. They're waiting for us. We gotta go."

———·••·———

Over the sound of clanging plates, I devoured the last bite of my strawberry shortcake and pushed the plate aside. Roxie rose from her chair, walked to the end of the table and turned to the other diners and began snapping her fingers as if to garner the attention of everyone. The bustling noise of a moment ago turned to silence. "Thank you all for coming to tonight's dinner event. Let me ask, how many of you are familiar with the history of the inn?"

All the hands in the room shot into the air.

"Good. Then let me tell you about some of the ghost stories you may not have heard." Roxie began, her voice low, deep, "I spoke to several members of the staff who say that late at night, while they are sitting alone at the front desk, the elevator comes down to the lobby. The doors open, and no one is there."

Her gaze scanned the faces of the crowd. "Then there is the story of the caretaker of the inn. He reported where he shut off all of the lights after everyone had gone to sleep. He began to leave the premises, then had to return when he noticed that all of the lights he shut off just moments before were now back on. This happened to him several times."

She took a step closer and leaned in for effect. "One night, the night before her wedding, a young woman staying in a room closest to the cemetery was awakened to find her wedding dress floating across the room," Roxie said as she swept her hand slowly to and fro in front of the awestruck group. "Aside from that, even more stories. Some brides have reported to staff that when they look in the mirror in their rooms, they see the reflection of another girl dressed in a bride's gown standing next to them. Others have reported that they will be sitting on their bed talking to their loved ones and then, right in front of their eyes, they will see the bed depressed as if someone was sitting beside them."

Inhaling deeply, she continued, "All of these stories come independently from people who knew nothing of the Lydia Carver story. Of course, Lydia's ghost is not just confined to the rooms. Many residents of the town as well as guests of the inn have reported seeing a woman dressed in white roaming the grounds."

One woman's gasp rose above the murmur of the group.

"Last, and perhaps the most terrifying, is the story that on a fog-filled night, some have heard blood-curdling screams on Crescent Beach. Are these the distraught voices of the drowning victims of the *Charles*?" Roxie lowered her voice and glanced toward our table. "Maybe tonight, we will find the answer.

"Does anyone have any questions?"

No one responded.

"Okay, everyone go back to your rooms. We're going to meet in the lobby in thirty minutes."

A half hour later, as we stood waiting for the rest of the group to assemble, I felt a tap on my shoulder.

"Are you Ron?" I turned and looked down at a lithe woman with a curious look in her eyes.

"Yes."

"I heard you were coming tonight, and I was glad that I was working, because I have my own story to share with you." Her voice rose in excitement. "My name is Erin. I've been working here for two years now. And ever since I started working here,

I have always had the feeling that someone is watching me." As if reliving the moment, she visibly shivered, then continued, "Regina told you about the elevator, right?"

"Yes."

"Well, late one night, while working the front desk, the elevator came down to the lobby, and when it opened, it was empty. I called out, 'Hello, is anyone there?' There was no response, but just then the calculator that was sitting on the desk beside me began running like someone was depressing the pound key over and over again. The weird thing about it is that it was shut off. The doors on the elevator closed, and at that very moment, the calculator stopped by itself. To this day, I still can't figure out what happened."

"Wow! That's interesting. Thank you for sharing that with us."

Roxie, who had walked over to join the conversation, responded, "Oooh, I've got another story to add to my repertoire."

Just then, Roxie bellowed over the encroaching crowd. "Everybody ready? Okay, let's go," she said as she motioned toward the dimly lit corridor that lay ahead of us. "This way."

With Maureen and me in the lead, I felt more like a mother duck than the lead investigator of the New England Ghost Project.

"Beep, beep, beep, beep . . ." Maureen's face became illuminated by the red glow of my borrowed EMF meter. One look at her face and I knew that she was about to channel.

"Maureen, are you okay?"

My question was met by deep, short gasps of breath, followed by a low, guttural moan as she stumbled toward the wall.

A concerned member of our party reached out to steady her.

I startled the group as I screamed, "No, leave her alone! Give her some space."

Bending at the waist, with hands on her thighs, she began to weep.

Roxie's voice rose an octave. "Look everyone, Maureen is actually channeling now."

Ignoring the sideshow and the horrified crowd, I turned to Maureen. "Who am I speaking with?"

Maureen raised her head. Through quivering voice, she whispered, "This is Lydia."

Addressing the spirit speaking through Maureen, I asked, "Lydia, why are you here?"

Suddenly choked up again, the spirit within spoke, "It's . . . because of me. Because of me . . ."

"Because of you what?"

"They're . . . they're all gone."

"You blame yourself?"

Maureen stumbled backward against the wall of the corridor, her body racked with sobs as her mascara ran in rivers down her cheeks.

My heart broke. The sad sight tugged at my heart strings. To think that Lydia had endured this self-inflicted guilt for two hundred years. I spoke up in her defense. "Lydia, it is not your fault. Don't blame yourself for the shipwreck. You weren't the captain." I waited for a moment to let my words sink in. "The captain is in charge of the ship. You were just a passenger." I reiterated, "It's not your fault."

With the last of my words, Maureen's sobbing subsided. I knew she was back among the living. So, I reached into my pocket to retrieve my neatly folded handkerchief and handed it to her. "Was that Lydia?"

Maureen continued to dab her eyes, her mascara blackening my nice white hanky.

"Why does she believe she's responsible for the wreck?"

"She feels responsible for the deaths of all those who were with her and the people around her. I don't know why." Maureen sniffled. "I feel like she's watching out for people when they stay here, especially the brides. She seems very emotionally attached to them."

Roxie took that moment to address the crowd. "And that is exactly what the folks at the inn describe. Most visitations from Lydia come from brides-to-be. And they are the ones who have the most vivid encounters with her as I described at dinner." Pausing for effect, she then continued, "There seems to be a strong emotional connection as Maureen described between Lydia and brides-to-be. Perhaps because she never had the chance to marry."

Roxie turned away from the crowd for a moment and glanced at Maureen. "It's funny that you would channel in this very spot, because there was a guest who reported seeing a translucent bride in this corridor. He followed her." Pointing to where Maureen was standing, she continued, "And she disappeared . . . just about there."

A collective gasp arose from the crowd.

Roxie motioned down the corridor. "Okay, let's check out one of the rooms where she has been seen."

Two by two like animals in Noah's Ark, we continued down the hall until we stopped at a door that led to one of the suites.

I knocked. "Trick or treat." The door slowly opened as laughter erupted behind me.

We filed into the room past Jan and Maureen's husband, Steve, filling the small space. "See what my wife does when I go on a ghost hunt? She has another man in my room."

Steve replied, "We're fully clothed."

"That's good to know."

One woman's voice rose above the chatter. "Roxie, you said Lydia has been seen by many brides staying in these rooms. How does she get in?"

"I really don't know. I can only surmise that she either passes through the door or the wall, but it is a frequent occurrence.

Oddly enough, many of the brides are not afraid of her. I feel bad for what Maureen is going through tonight, but I feel that there is so much emotion with [Lydia] and she is feeding off the energy of the group. Maybe she senses we are curious about her and she wants her story told."

"Poor Lydia."

Maureen responded to the woman, "I know. I feel bad for her too, but I don't believe she's here with us now."

Following Maureen's lead, I said, "Okay, well, if she's not here, let's go upstairs to the dining room."

As we entered the dining room, I pointed to the pristine white wedding dress hanging off a coat hook. "Here's the wedding dress."

Roxie piped up. "Did your wife leave it there, or did Lydia put it there?"

"No, Jan did. I haven't seen that dress in thirty-five years."

A woman from the back of the room spoke up, "Does it still fit?"

"Me?" I chuckled. "No! But I've gained a few pounds since then."

Maureen tugged at my arm, "Actually, I can feel energy. I feel Lydia around us right now."

No sooner had her words left her lips than my borrowed EMF meter began to blare. I gazed at the meter and thought, *Damn, I wish I knew what happened to my meter. I know I packed it.*

I turned my attention back to the crowd. "Can anyone feel anything?"

The lady who had asked the previous question said, "I feel the hairs on the back of my neck standing up."

Another voice came from the crowd: "I have a headache."

"Good. These manifestations all occur when spirit is around. Everyone's experience can be unique. Some experience headaches, while others have reported feeling a tightness in their chest."

"My camera batteries just died, and I had put new ones in when we started," another voice chimed in.

"That's not uncommon either when you do paranormal investigating. There is a theory that spirits use the batteries' energy to do what they do."

"I can hear Lydia now," Maureen said. "I think she wants us to go outside."

"To visit her grave?" Roxie asked.

"Yes, I feel she does," Maureen said.

I spoke up, "Everybody grab your coats. We're going outside." I glanced at my wrist. "It's getting late and it is February. It's going to be freakin' cold out there, guys."

A few people laughed. A couple grumbled. *Oh well, this is the life of a ghost hunter. Deal with it.*

———·•·———

Within minutes, we were all standing in a circle around the oversized granite tombstone engraved with an urn and a weeping willow.

While the crowd huddled in a hushed silence, Roxie began to read the epitaph:

> *Sacred*
> *To the memory of*
> *Miss Lydia Carver*
> *daut'r of Mr. Amis Carver of Freeport*
> *AE 21 who with 15 other unfortunate*
> *passengers male and female perished*
> *in the merciless waves by the shipwreck*
> *of the schooner Charles Capt. Jacob Adams*
> *bound from Boston to Portland*
> *on a reef of rocks near the shore of*
> *Richmond's Island on Sunday night*
> *July 12, 1807*

In a moment of sentiment, Roxie ran her fingers atop the carving, caressing the cold stone. Her voice grew stronger, more intense. "Take a look around you at the other graves," she said as she gestured toward the darkness. "Even though Lydia's gravestone is nearly two hundred years old and one of the oldest ones here, it is by far the nicest. And it's in amazing shape. Some believe that it's in such good shape because Lydia herself tends to it."

"Roxie, can I take a picture of the grave?"

"Please do."

Click. Click. Click.

The woman looked at the screen on the camera. "Oh, my God. Look at this!" she exclaimed.

A second woman peering over her shoulder shouted, "What is that?" She stepped forward shoving the camera in my face. "Ron, what is that?"

"Looks like an orb to me."

"Some people believe that's spirit energy, you know," Roxie answered.

Almost immediately, the darkness was shattered by flashes of light as several people began to take pictures of Lydia's grave.

No longer able to feel my fingers, I decided to wrap it up. "I have a great idea. Let's all head back into the lobby where it's warm. We can look at the pictures there."

The crusted snow crunched beneath our feet as we walked back.

The heat of the fireplace never felt so good as the blood slowly returned to my nose.

For the next fifteen minutes or so, like kids on Christmas morning, the guests shared the pictures of the numerous orbs they'd captured. As the excitement waned and the hours dwindled, I thought it was time I addressed the crowd. "I want to thank everyone for coming tonight, and I hope you had a good time. But I think it's time to call it a night."

I waited for the crowd to dissipate and then headed back to my room. Opening the door, I snuck in quietly so as not to wake Jan and began putting my equipment away.

"Oh, my God!"

The bed creaked behind me. "What? What's the matter Ron?" Jan spoke in a half-awakened voice. "You okay?"

"You're not gonna believe this! I stuck my hand in the pocket of my duffel bag to put away my equipment, and my freakin' EMF meter is there." My mind reeled. *How the hell is that possible?*

Jan replied, her voice lacking enthusiasm. "That's nice, Ronnie. Now come to bed."

OUR THOUGHTS

MAUREEN:

Although our communication with Lydia Carver was a brief one, I couldn't help but have a heavy heart. The gravity of loss and guilt she'd endured for nearly two centuries is inconceivable. It's my experience that just as in life, it is also in death. This means when we are hurt or angry, and we voice it, when we release the emotion, we tend to feel lighter. By allowing Lydia an opportunity to voice the self-imposed guilt she's carried, it's my hope that she has now found the peace that she so rightly deserves.

RON:

This was an enjoyable dinner event with a great back story: the tragic story of the ghost bride. Besides having a great time, I thought the most fascinating event of the evening was the teleportation of my EMF meter. To this day, I have never been able to explain what happened that night. But what I can say is that I have experienced it several times since then.

A Sea Captain, a Drunken Sailor, and a Nice Old Lady

Case File: 1905863 A Sea Captain, a Drunken Sailor, and a Nice Old Lady

Location: Biddeford Pool, Maine

History: Biddeford Pool is the site of Maine's first recorded permanent settlement, which originally was named Winter Harbor. The first village was established in 1688. To this day, Wood Island Lighthouse, located a mile offshore, stands as a beacon for fishermen and lobstermen, directing them in to a safe harbor.

Reported Paranormal Activity: Strange sounds, ghostly images, and moving objects.

Clients: Sheri (FOWIL, Friends of Wood Island Lighthouse), Sandra (lobster pound owner).

Investigators: Ron (lead investigator), Maureen (trance medium).

Press: N/A.

Purpose of Investigation: A presentation for a FOWIL fundraiser and a mini investigation.

*T*hrough the thunderous clapping, Sheri made her way to the podium in the dimly lit old Union Church. Ron took a step to the side, half his face lit as the colors from the projector reflected off it, *casting an eerie shadow. Sheri glanced at us, her smile revealing her satisfaction with our presentation. She turned back to the packed church, adjusted the microphone lower, and began, "That was a great presentation. Thank you, Ron and Maureen. Because of your efforts, the Friends of Wood Island Lighthouse raised the necessary funds for the next phase in the restoration of the lighthouse.*

"And also, thank you all for coming tonight and for your continued support of our group. Be sure to take one of our tours to the island. Call to reserve your spot, so you don't miss out."

As the overhead lights grew brighter, the applause grew louder.

I swear Ron was blushing. Nahhh. What was I thinking? Blushing's not in his DNA.

Amid the sounds of people chatting, we were approached by Sean, one of the captains of the Light runner, the boat that took us out to the island nearly a year before.

"Maureen, I got to show you something," he raised his voice to be heard above the chatter. "I was taking pictures tonight during your presentation, and I got this one." Flicking through the pictures on his professional-quality digital camera, he said, "Do you have any idea what this might be?"

Amazing. "That's kind of interesting, because when I first walked in, I sensed the presence of a sea captain." I glanced at Ron, who was finishing a conversation with another enthusiastic guest. I waited for a moment, then said, "Hey, Ron. Got a minute? What do you think of this?" pointing to the screen of Sean's camera.

Ron stared at the image for a moment. "That's pretty cool."

Sean raised his eyes and stuttered, "Do you think this blue mist behind Maureen could be something paranormal?"

"Geez, it could be." Ron grabbed his chin. "Didn't you pick up on a sea captain when we first arrived?"

"Yeah. He's been hovering around us all night."

Ron chuckled. "Well, I hope he enjoyed the presentation."

We were soon joined by a young man who stood quietly by. "Hello, Ron. My name is Harold Rosenberg. I'd like to ask you something."

"Sure, how can I help you?'

"Have you ever heard of Thomas Glendenning Hamilton?"

"It rings a bell, but I can't put my finger on it."

"Well, he was a famous paranormal researcher back in the thirties. And he is also my wife's grandfather."

"Wow, that's pretty cool."

"His entire collection of evidential research is housed in a special wing at the University of Manitoba in Canada." *He continued,* "But my wife has a bunch of photos he took during the séance sessions. Would you be interested in seeing them?"

Ron's grin grew wide as he replied, "Is the Pope Catholic?"

I thought to myself, This is unbelievable. This could be life changing. For so many years, there have been so many people who have doubted my abilities. This could be the proof in existence of spirit communication that I've been looking for. *I joined the conversation.* "I, for one, am totally excited to see them!"

"Great. I have to go to Canada to get them. When I return, I'll give you a call. It may be a week or two."

Ron pulled a business card from his wallet and handed it to Harold. "Give me a call when you get back."

Sheri interrupted our conversation. "I hate to do this to you guys, but we have to get going."

After we finished putting the equipment in the trunk, we followed Sheri to the lobster pound.

I stepped out of the car and the ground crunched loudly beneath my feet. "What the heck?"

"Don't you know they use shells for paving in sea towns?" *Ron said.*

"Apparently not."

A tall, broad-shouldered woman stepped through the side door and approached us. "Hi, Sheri." *She then turned to us.* "You must *be Ron and Maureen. Sheri's told me all about you. My name is Sandra."*

I glanced at Sheri. "All? Now I'm nervous."

Sheri chuckled and Ron spoke up, "So what's going on here?"

"I feel like I'm being watched. Sometimes I swear I can see something out of the corner of my eye." She pushed her bangs behind her ears and continued, "I'm forever hearing footsteps, and when I look, there's no one there. And every time that door slams for no reason, it just drives me crazy."

"So do you think the building's haunted?" Ron asked.

"I don't know. I'm hoping you can tell me." Without waiting for a response, Sandra did an about-face and led us into the building.

As I passed through the screen door, I could immediately sense the presence of a woman. Her energy flirted with me and was confirmed by the sporadic readings from Ron's EMF meter.

"That's weird." Ron looked down at his meter. "Here one minute, gone the next."

"I can feel the presence of a woman here, but it's fleeting. It feels as if she comes close, then pulls back just as quickly."

"Is she shy?" Ron asked. "Or is she playing games?"

"Not sure. But whoever she is, her energy feels sweet. Certainly, nothing to be worried about."

"Is she related to me?" Sandra interjected.

I took a moment to focus on the energy that was hovering as I attempted to get a better reading.

"No, I don't think so."

The wide-plank pine floor creaked beneath our feet as we journeyed from room to room with similar results. "Well, that's it," Sandra said, "unless you want to go into the basement. That's where I feel like I'm being watched."

The words sank in as my mind began to conjure up nightmarish visions of spiders and cobwebs. Ewww, I thought to myself, I can hardly wait.

Ron flashed a grin in my direction. He knows I hate spiders.

"Sure, we'll go." He laughed. "Come on, Maureen. You can speak to the dead, but you're afraid of an itsy-bitsy little spider."

"Itsy bitsy, my ass."

Bending over, Sandra tugged on the large metal ring resting atop the floor to no avail.

"This darn humidity," she grumbled as she pulled harder. The hatch gave way with a large groan, exposing a set of rickety stairs to the basement.

I leaned over the opening. "Oh, that looks pleasant."

"Will you stop whining?!"

We descended the fragile stairs into the bowels of the building, manipulating our way through a maze of low-hanging pipes and large metal tanks filled with water. I could only assume it was for the fresh catch of the day.

Just as I was about to speak, I felt her. The energy that had been fleeting was now growing stronger by the second. I reached in my pocket and pulled out my pendulum.

"Whatcha gettin'?" Ron asked.

"She's very sweet." I looked past Ron to Sandra.

"Really? Who is she?"

"I'm getting that she was a spinster. She likes your smile and thinks you're a good person." I closed my eyes to focus. "That's why she likes to hang around here. It seems she has adopted you."

Sandra covered her heart with her hand and smiled. Her eyes wet with tears, she replied, "That really makes me feel good."

"There's nothing to worry about. She really likes you."

"Well, ain't that just special," Ron quipped.

No sooner had he spoken than I nearly burst out laughing at the sudden image in my mind's eye.

"What are you laughing about?"

"I could see the little old lady wagging a bony finger at you as she said, 'I've heard about you.'"

"Really? I guess my joke about my picture hanging in the post office of the spirit world is not so far off from the truth."

Sandra asked, "Does she have anything else to say?"

"It seems not; her energy is dissipating rapidly. She's gone. I think she just wanted to set your mind at ease. Don't worry, she'll be back."

"You know, Maureen, I think we're going to have to go now. It's getting late, and we still have to go over to the general store before our long ride home."

"It's always a long ride home." I choked back a laugh as Ron miscalculated his height and banged his head on the floor joist as he ascended the stairs.

As we reached the parking lot, Sandra leaned in and gave me a big hug. "Maureen, I want to thank you so much. I feel so much better now."

"Glad we could help. Have a good night."

It took longer to climb into the car than it did to get to our next destination—the general store that was located across the street. Although there were only five weathered steps to the porch of the store, after the presentation and the investigation at the lobster pound, it seemed as if we were climbing the Empire State Building. The metal bell clanged, announcing our arrival as we entered through the screen door.

We stood for a moment assessing our surroundings and absorbing the old-fashioned ambiance of the building. Before us stood aisle after aisle of wooden shelves stocked with packaged foods, candy, first-aid, and sundries. All the same products as the major supermarkets but in much smaller quantities. The one-stop shop for Biddeford Pool. It was as if we'd stepped back in time.

Sheri called out to the man standing behind a small counter and introduced us.

I followed Ron down the wine aisle toward the back of the store. As I drew closer to the end of the aisle, the energy that I'd barely sensed upon walking in grew stronger and stronger. "Hey, Ron. Here. I can feel someone now."

"Here? That's so funny. I felt something in this exact spot when I was here the other day. But you know me. What do I know?"

I couldn't help but think that Ron was more psychic than he wanted to admit. "Yeah, I forgot. You're the dumb psychic."

I continued a couple of steps on the old wide-plank pine floor till I reached the Pinot Grigio aisle. "The spirit's really strong here. No pun intended." I crack myself up.

"Do you want to communicate?"

"Sure," I said reluctantly, feeling the weight of the night's events. I reached into my pocket and pulled out my brass pendulum. "Is there anyone here with us?"

The pendulum immediately began to swing. Yes.

Suddenly, the room began sway to and fro. Oh no . . .

As I looked into Maureen's eyes, her blank stare told me all I needed to know. She was no longer there.

"Maureen! Maureen, are you all right?"

The only reply was the swaying of her body back and forth. "Who am I speaking with?"

She raised her head and stumbled backward. Her arm went limp as the pendulum crashed to the floor.

"Who am I speaking with?"

In a slurred Irish brogue, she muttered, "I want . . . a drink." *Seriously. This was a first.*

"I'll make you a deal. You answer my questions, and I'll give you a drink. Are you a sailor?"

"Sure. My drink now."

"Not yet." *Oh great. A drunken sailor. This ain't going nowhere.* "Who are you?"

"I want a drink." Maureen gurgled. "Give me my drink, you bloke."

Enough of this. "Maureen, come back. Push him out."

After stumbling about for a couple of minutes more, she regained her consciousness. "What the hell? My head is killing me."

"Well, you probably have a hangover."

"Not funny, Ron. I think I've had enough."

"Me, too. Let's call it quits."

I looked behind me at Sheri, who stood there stunned. Even though she'd seen Maureen channel before, seeing her channel a drunken sailor might have been just a bit too much. "I think we're going to call it a night, Sheri. We really appreciate it, but I think we've had it."

"I totally understand. We just can't thank you enough for all you've done for the Friends of Wood Island Lighthouse."

"It was our pleasure." And with that, we headed out to the car and embarked on our two-hour journey home.

OUR THOUGHTS

MAUREEN:

Sean's picture of the blue mist taken during our presentation for FOWIL was awesome. Feeling the presence of a spirit only to have it validated a short time later helps to keep the "Am I crazy" thoughts from winning. Having said that, I was looking forward to finally having the opportunity to come face to face with research that could prove the existence of life after death. Could you imagine? Wouldn't it be nice if there was evidence to validate that mediums were real and NOT charlatans (at least not all of us) as some might think? Unfortunately, this was not to be, when several weeks later we received the collection of evidential research that had been housed at the University of Manitoba in Canada. I eagerly viewed it with Ron. Instead of validating that mediums were not frauds, it almost contributed to the opposite. Instead of mediums connecting with spirits, the images appeared to display cardboard cutouts (ghosts), cotton balls hanging from the mediums' lips (ectoplasm), and so on. While the images were cool in that they were from the early twentieth century, my hopes were dashed. These were not going to be the validation for all mediums I'd hoped for. Don't give up. There is hope yet.

RON:

It was a rewarding night for me. Not only did we help raise over $5,000 for the Friends of Wood Island Lighthouse, we also got to do a mini investigation in town. (To read more about this fundraising event, view this link: *http://woodislandlighthouse.org/index.php/about/ghosts-of-wood-island/*.) It was the first time I saw Maureen drunk (even if she was just channeling), but I also discovered that through years of investigation, you can acquire a reputation on the other side. This event also gave me the chance to see firsthand photographs taken in the 1930s by paranormal researcher Thomas Glendenning Hamilton during his recorded séance sessions.

The Keeper

Case File: 1906890 The Moultonborough house

Location: Moultonborough, New Hampshire

History: The cottage was built in the 18th century by the Richardsons, the founding fathers of Moultonborough. It was then owned by the Hoyts and then purchased by the Lamprey family.

Reported Paranormal Activity: Apparitions, unexplained odors, an uneasiness, and the feeling of being watched.

Clients: Evelyn Lamprey (homeowner).

Investigators: Ron (lead investigator), Maureen (trance medium), Ron Jr. (investigator), Jim (photographer), Clay (tech manager).

Press: N/A.

Purpose of Investigation: To investigate the home of a *Ghost Chronicles* listener.

I returned from the gym, sat down at the desk, and turned on my computer. I'd been away for only a couple of hours but was already eager to check my messages. I clicked on Outlook and watched the parade of emails stream by me. Through the usual spam and other requests, one caught my eye. I opened it and read:

To: Ron Kolek   Today: 3:45 PM

Dear Ron and Maureen, I have been listening to your podcast for the last few months and have learned quite a bit. That fact that it is a New England based program is really appealing to me. I'm hoping that if you have time, you might be able to help me out. I'd like to find out more about what's going on in a house I have up in Moultonborough. I wrote everything down a few months ago and here's an excerpt: 38 years ago, my family inherited an old cape from my great aunt, who had owned it since the [1920s]. Though built in the late 18th century, it had been owned by only two other families before my great aunt purchased it. The first family, the Richardsons, founded the town, and the second were the Hoyts. The house had never been updated, which from a historical perspective was wonderful, as many of the original architectural features were still intact; however it had no running water and a very rudimentary electrical system. There was no insulation to speak of, and there was quite a bit of wood rot—you get the picture. My parents were very handy and wanted to do much of the restoration work themselves. Dad started working on the house every night after work; much of the damaged wood in the floors had to be removed, and there was a lot of trash in the house that had to be burned.

One night, Dad, a very stolid, no-nonsense Yankee, was working in one of the rooms while staying warm with a roaring fire in the fireplace. Suddenly he felt the temperature drop dramatically, and the atmosphere changed—he said it was like being in a room with someone who was really pissed at him. The feeling intensified to the point where he had to run out of the house, leaving all the lights on and the fire still going. From then on he couldn't work there alone; he and Mom worried that they wouldn't be able to live in the house after it was finished. However, as the construction project turned from tearing things apart to putting them back together, Dad noted that the house became "friendlier" and he never had another similar experience.

[Fifteen] years later, a friend of mine from college was staying with my parents while he looked for work. In exchange for a room, he would work on the guest house—my great aunt named it the "Winnibanana," since Lake Winnipesaukee is right down the street—the cottage was in a pretty sad state and needed a lot of work. Part of the project included tearing down a little kitchen ell which had partially collapsed. One day I came over to visit; he seemed bothered by something, and he took me aside to describe what happened that day while working on the cabin when my parents were out. He was tearing apart the ell and suddenly felt as though someone was there watching him. He didn't see anyone, so he went outside and looked around, still saw no one. He became increasingly uncomfortable, to the point where he walked down the street to the beach (about a tenth of a mile), where the feeling of discomfort finally stopped. He didn't come back to the house until he saw my parents' car pull in. He walked back up, feeling much less agitated. He didn't tell my parents about it, worried that they'd think he was nuts.

I had never told him any stories about the house, and he was a little miffed that I hadn't mentioned it before he came to stay there. It didn't happen again as he wouldn't work unless my parents were home! Based on this incident and my Dad's initial problems in the house, I guess the spirit doesn't like change, or hates construction projects. Another spirit in the house has never appeared to anyone in my family, only to guests. Maybe she is the same as described above but the general contention is that she is a second, more friendly spirit—perhaps you can shed some light on this. Several neighbors and friends have described seeing a woman with brown hair and a long dress, apparently a full body apparition. She appeared in the bedroom doorway while my tough Texan relative was reading—he said at first he thought it was his wife, but then heard her voice downstairs. He didn't tell anyone until we started swapping ghost stories one evening a few days later, after several cocktails. He said that she appeared to be quite solid, easily mistaken for a living person.

A related incident occurred when my parents let a young couple do laundry at the house: one night Mom and Dad came home after an evening out to find the two of them huddled in front of the tiny TV in the summer kitchen (a later addition to the house). Dad asked why they didn't watch the big TV in the family room—they said that the summer kitchen was the only room the lady ghost would let them use! They were very scared to go beyond the doorway from the kitchen to the rest of the house, having seen the woman and feeling very uncomfortable. The young man then went on to tell them that he had seen her in the house several times, in the parlor and the front kitchen (an 1825 addition). The woman is often seen in the parlor and some people feel uncomfortable there, though it is otherwise a bright and pleasant area. Interestingly, there is a secret room built into the chimney, approximately 4 × 4 feet, accessible from the parlor. It's always been called the "Indian hiding hole," but I'm not sure where the name originated.

My family has been both disappointed and relieved that we have never seen this ghost—we were never sure why we hadn't seen her and a sighting would certainly confirm the stories. I guess I don't have to believe it if I haven't seen her—I can delude myself into thinking that I don't share the house with anyone.

The last experience, about 5 years ago, was the most powerful and positive. My mother had terminal cancer and wanted to die at home. We made sure that her last week was as comfortable and pleasant as possible. All of her friends and family came to see her; she told us what she wanted for a memorial service (a big party with lots of food, and friends telling stories about her—bagpipes if we could get them!) and that we shouldn't be upset, because she was at peace and ready to go. She finally died at around 9 a.m., with Dad, my sister, a neighbor and [me] right there with her. Afterward, Dad went out to the kitchen to take a breather and the three of us tidied up to stay busy and not fall apart. About 20 minutes after she died, I walked into her bedroom and suddenly there was the most amazing, powerful, heady smell of flowers filling the room—it smelled like a garden after a rainstorm, or on a humid morning in the summer. Really intense. Given that all the flower arrangements in the room were on their last legs, there was no way to explain it. My sister and neighbor came into the room and smelled it immediately. The feeling in the room was so exciting and happy; exhilarating. I quickly went to the other end of the house to get Dad so he could come experience it, but the fragrance followed me all the way there! Dad said, "It smells like someone spilled a whole bottle of perfume in the room!" It lasted another 5 minutes or so, and then was completely gone.

Sadly, my father committed suicide last summer. He also had terminal cancer and didn't want to suffer anymore. He was very depressed. I did not have an experience like the one with Mom upon his passing, I only wish I had, to be sure that he was finally happy and at peace. Currently I have a contractor working at the house, and a divorcé in the guest house who has seen the ghost several times when visiting over the years. He recently asked the contractor if he's seen the ghost—no sightings yet, much to the contractor's disappointment, as my tenant described her as "hot." I have attached two images of the house taken this winter. I look forward to hearing from you and hope that you can make a trip up to Moultonborough.

Regards,

Evelyn L.

Picking up the receiver, I dialed Maureen's number.

"Hi, Ron. What's up?"

"What, are you psychic?"

"About as psychic as a caller ID."

"Hey, I received an email from one of our listeners. She loves the show. But that's not why she wrote."

"Okay. So, what did she want?"

"She inherited an old farmhouse that she grew up in. It's supposed to be haunted, even though she's never seen anything. Till now, that is."

"So, what does she want?" I heard her say over the splash of water and clanging of metal.

"Are you doing the dishes?"

"Just multitasking." She chuckled. "What, are you psychic?"

"Ha-ha. Psychic as a brick."

I continued, "Anyways, she just wants us to investigate. She's looking for validation. We should go. How can we resist a fan?"

"Yeah, right. When?"

"The last Saturday of the month. Okay?"

"Yeah, fine. I think I'm free. I'll mark it on the calendar."

When the day finally arrived, I showed up at Maureen's house with Jim and Ron Jr. We found Maureen waiting, leaning against her car. As soon as our car door opened, Maureen called out, "We're taking my car."

"Shotgun," I said, as I jumped in the passenger side seat. *More legroom.* Jim and Ron Jr. piled into the back, and we were on our way.

Mere minutes down the road, Maureen spoke up, "You know, Ron. I know we get a lot of requests for help, but why did you pick the one that was two or three hours' away?"

"Well, I had divine guidance."

"Divine guidance, my ass," she said, rolling her eyes.

"Don't worry. I'm sure we will be there by Christmas."

Maureen's voice grew louder. "I am going to open the door and throw you out, and then I'll be communicating with you next."

"Whatever." *Oh boy, this was going to be a long ride.* You know, it's raining. There's traffic. And intermittent windshield wipers are nice, but if you put them on like regular, they actually clean the windows. I'm just sayin'."

"Hey, listen, my husband went away for a week, and I'm on vacation." She paused, then emphasized, "I don't want another nag. Sorry."

"A nag? That's not me. It is not in my nature."

"Really?"

Maureen pointed to the car that cut us off in traffic. "Oh, look—3333. Four threes on the license plate!"

"What does that mean?"

"The ascended angels and masters are with us. Remember when we talked about Doreen Virtue's angel numbers. Well, that's what the threes stand for."

"Yikes! A cop car."

"Don't worry. I'm protected. He didn't even see us."

"Okay, but somehow I disagree."

"Don't forget, I have my paranormal posse. Remember that?"

"Oh yeah, some psychic medium told you that you have a crowd of spirits behind you that help you."

"Yup, that's right."

"Humph." Maureen glanced in my direction. What?"

"Please tell me you're not recording this conversation."

"What makes you say that?"

"Because I know you. So turn that damn thing off," she said as she turned up the radio volume.

I gritted my teeth and sat quietly for the remainder of the ride, much as Jim and Ron Jr. had the entire trip.

———————

No sooner had we stepped out of Maureen's car than the two mimes in the backseat spoke up, "Damn guys, you two sound like an old married couple."

"Eww." Maureen grimaced.

The screen door opened on the red cottage before us. A woman with dark hair approached. "Hi, I'm Evelyn. I'm really excited you could make it."

Just then, we could hear the kicking up of gravel as Clay, the newest member of our team, arrived in his new white Toyota Tundra. He rolled down the driver's side window. "Hey, Ron."

"Hey, Clay. Can you take Ron Jr. and set up base camp?"

Over the commotion of Ron and Clay grabbing equipment, we turned our attention back to Evelyn.

Evelyn spoke up, "You know, Ron, the founders of the town are buried just down the street from here. You feel like taking a walk?"

I turned toward Maureen. "What do you think?"

"Fine with me."

"Guys," I yelled through the screen door. "Finish setting up base camp. We'll be back in a couple of minutes."

While we walked down the hill to the cemetery, we continued our conversation. "Evelyn, what do you expect to get out of this investigation?"

"Illumination. I want a better idea of who this woman is that people have seen. If there is more than one. If they like it here. If they're happy and well. If I can live with them."

"Coexist?"

"Yes, can we coexist?"

We squeezed our way through the stone wall that surrounded the cemetery and began to wander to and fro among the weathered gravestones.

Evelyn pointed to a slightly leaning tombstone. "Here is Bradbury's grave. He was one of the founders of the town. He and his brother built my house and another house just like it about a mile and a half away."

"Your house is really historic. Built by one of the founding fathers. Wow! So, Richardson was the first owner?" I asked.

"Yes, Richardson, then Hoyt, then my Great Aunt Evelyn bought it, and when she died, she left it to my father. I have lived in it for about thirty-five years."

"Evelyn, I think the woman who has been seen at your house is buried here," Maureen said.

"Oh, really?"

"Yes," she said as she stopped walking and closed her eyes as if concentrating. "That's weird. I hear the name Emily." Maureen continued to stumble among the stones until she stood in front of a large piece of moss-covered slate. "I think this is it."

"Really?" I said as I quickly ran to the other side and stooped to see if I could find the name. I glanced up over the stone to Maureen and read the name, "Emelia Richardson."

"Hmmm? Emilia. It's a little bit off." Maureen closed her eyes and concentrated for a moment. "I hear them say, they called me Em. . . ."

"M like Mulder? Maureen?" I replied.

"No. Em, like Emelia."

"Ahhh. Emilia Richardson. That does make sense."

I glanced down at Evelyn. "What's your take? Do you think it's her?

Without hesitation, she responded. "I have no preconception. That is why I contacted you. It could be someone from this graveyard. I really don't know."

"The funny thing is that if someone sees a spirit in the house, they just assume it is someone who died there. There are some spirits that seem to be connected with the house or property, while others are in visitation. They can come and go," I said.

"You mean the spirits are from somewhere else?"

"It could be any or all of the above."

"Both my parents died of cancer in the house. I know my father committed suicide, but it is really the cancer that killed him. But I don't feel either one of them there."

My eyes began to water. "One of the reasons I took this case is that my wife is dealing with cancer. When I read about your parents, I knew that there was a message for me here somewhere."

"Sorry to hear your wife is not well."

"Thank you, but I think we should head back. The boys must be done setting up the equipment by now." For some reason, the walk back felt shorter; maybe it was our enthusiasm over discovering the gravestone. Either way, we were back in a flash.

When we returned, we were met by a tall, thin man with a goatee.

"Ron, this is Jeff. He's the tenant of the guest house. He can tell you a little bit about his experiences here."

"Sure, I'd be glad to. I've been friends with the family for years. Kind of like an adopted stepson. Eventually, I moved into their rental property across the street with my girlfriend. It was very uncomfortable for us to go into the home except the front kitchen, and I can remember many a night sitting in the parlor with the goose bumps and that creepy feeling like someone was staring at you and didn't want you there.

"One day in January I was out of work, so I came by to have coffee with Pat, Evelyn's mother. She excused herself to use the bathroom. I was sitting in the chair, and I heard someone in the kitchen. I thought Evelyn had come home from school, so I got up to say hello. When I went into the kitchen, I saw a woman shuffling about. I watched her for about fifteen seconds. She never acknowledged me, but she was as real as you are. Then as quickly as she appeared, she disappeared."

"Do you remember what she looked like?"

"Yes, she was tall and slender, very beautiful with long black hair. And the really odd part about this was that she was wearing a light, flowered, summer dress, which was weird since it was about ten below outside."

"Is there anything else you want to tell us?"

"Yes, I built a shop in the house across the street. One day I was working in it when I caught the odor of something flowery like perfume. I looked all around and couldn't find the source. It happened several times. I finally asked my girlfriend about it. She said she smelled it in the house before. She said it was the exact odor they all smelled when Evelyn's mother died. I still get a whiff of it from time to time."

"Thanks for the information, Dave. That's pretty cool. And we appreciate your time."

The three of us walked back into the house and entered the parlor, which was chock-full of memorabilia. A picture of a steamship on the mantel caught my eye. I walked over to it for a closer look. "So, Evelyn, your family goes way back in town, huh? Isn't that your family name on the steamship?"

"Yes, my family ran three steamships up here. My great aunt who bought this house in the twenties used to run booze out of it. In fact, people would come up from Boston and sleep here. There were beds from one end of the house to the other. It would cost them a dollar a night."

As Evelyn spoke about the history, Maureen interjected.

"I'm getting the feeling of a presence that might be your great aunt. She's telling me that she was there to help your mother when she passed."

Evelyn's voice began to quiver as tears filled her eyes. "I'm sorry. I didn't think I would be this emotional."

Maureen placed her hand to her chest. "Evelyn, who had something with their throat and lungs?"

"Mom." She sniffled.

"Okay. When I was sitting here, I was having a hard time with my breathing. My lungs felt tight. Constricted. I could feel like I was going to start coughing and choking."

"Yes, Mom had a terrible lung operation and breast cancer. She ended up in a coma and got pneumonia. I slept in her room all night, and I was right there when she went." Her sniffles turned to sobs.

I reached out and patted Evelyn's shoulder. "It's okay. She's not in pain anymore. She's fine now."

Maureen added, "When we starting talking about her, I could feel the energy get stronger. I think she knows what we do."

"She would have loved it," Evelyn said as she dabbed a tissue to her eyes.

"Evelyn, she's okay. Really. She doesn't want you to feel bad." In a comforting gesture, Maureen placed her hand on Evelyn's arm. "I could feel her reaching out to touch you, to comfort you. Your mom wants you to know that she comes back to visit. She hears you, so you can talk to her." Maureen smiled. "Sometimes tears aren't bad. Are you sure you're okay?"

"Yes, I'm good." Evelyn's voice sounded lighter, less weighted. "You guys ready to rock?"

"Yeah, we're ready." A thought crossed my mind. "Evelyn, did she do a lot of gardening?"

"She did. In fact, her ashes are out in the peonies. She was very specific about where she wanted to go. I can show you the exact spot."

" I would love to see that. Can you do it now?

"Absolutely!"

"Maureen, do you want to come with us."

"No, thanks. I think I'll stay here."

As the screen door banged behind me, I called back to Maureen, "Don't do anything I wouldn't do."

The leaves crunched beneath our feet as we walked around the side of the house and into the backyard. Evelyn's gait slowed as we approached a small patch of greenery, the remains of what appeared to have been a flower garden. She stopped. "Here it is."

"Oh, wow."

She raised her right hand and gestured to a small clearing in the side yard. "We had a big tent over there. A big party with all of her friends. And at the end of the day, after everyone left, I spread her ashes here."

"Why do you think she picked this spot?"

"She loved to garden. She loved the smell of peonies. And she absolutely loved this house."

As we stood in silence, I couldn't help but think that the odor that Dave and his wife had experienced was a calling card from Pat. It was her way of letting them know that she was still there.

We returned to the house, where Maureen joined us. Evelyn led us to a good-sized bedroom just off to the left of the living room. "This is the room my mother died in. In fact, I have something for both of you." Bending at the waist, she pulled a large storage container filled with books from beneath the bed. She lifted it off the floor and gently placed it on the comforter. Her eyes glistened with tears as she removed the cover and reached inside. "These were my mother's favorite books. I really want you to have them."

"That's very sweet of you, but are you sure?" Maureen said.

"Absolutely. Mom's friends asked about them, but something tells me that she would have wanted you guys to have them."

"Well, thank you very much," we said in unison.

"Maureen, why don't we take a few minutes to go through them?"

Evelyn's smile grew wide. "I'm so happy that you'll enjoy them. Okay, I'll see you in a couple of minutes."

With Evelyn gone, Maureen and I shuffled through the container of books, selecting the titles we each wanted. When we were through, we placed them in neat, short stacks on the bed.

The grumble in my stomach made me realize the time. The hands on my watch confirmed it. It was dinner time. "Maureen, why don't we leave these here for now? Let's go get everyone and grab some dinner. We still have a long night ahead."

We left the room, securing the door behind us. "Evelyn, we're going to go get something to eat. Do you want to go with us?"

"I'd love to, but I have something to do tonight. Be sure to lock the house if you leave."

We said our good-byes, and we each went our separate ways.

————·————

With our stomachs filled, we returned an hour later.

Ron unlocked the front door, and I darted past him and headed to the bedroom. Like a kid in a candy store, I found myself eager to take another look at the books. I pushed open the bedroom door and froze. "Ron, come in here quick!"

A mere moment later, Ron was standing beside me.

"All right, look at this! Remember, we left these books piled up neatly on the bed. Now look at them. They're all over the floor. . . ."

Ron's voice rose an octave. "Get out. That's crazy."

He continued. "Wait! Don't touch them. I want to take a picture."

Ron circled the bed, stepping over the books littering the floor. He paused by the window. Taking out his camera, he raised it to his eye and pressed the shutter. "That's bizarre."

"Are your batteries dying?"

"Hold on. Let me take another picture. You're right. My batteries are dying," Ron said as he began to fiddle with the camera.

"Holy shit . . . take a look at this! There's the floor, and there are no books in the picture."

I peered at the camera screen and couldn't believe what I was seeing. I pointed. "Oh, my God! There is the corner of the bureau, but there's nothing on the floor. How is that possible?" I continued, "We are looking at the books on the floor, but there's nothing in the picture . . ."

"My batteries are dead. I've got to put new ones in and take another picture. I need to figure out what the hell is going on." Ron pulled new AAs out of his jacket pocket and placed them in the camera. He held it to his eye again and clicked.

"Now that's bizarre," he said as he held the camera up for me to see. "Look, you can see the books in this picture."

"How freakin' weird is that?!"

Ron Jr. poked his head in the doorway, "We're all set up for the table tipping experiment in the parlor. We're ready when you are."

TABLE TIPPING

The manipulation of a table during a séance as a method of spirit communication.

As we walked into the parlor, Ron stopped short at the mantel, picking up a little glass jar. He brought it to his nose and took a whiff of the dried, leafy mixture. He grimaced. "Ooh. What is this stuff?"

I grabbed the jar from Ron's hand. "It's got rosemary, lavender, and something else, maybe sage."

"So it's potpourri?"

"No, I think it's some type of protection."

"So, Pat's Special Blend?"

I could tell by the look on Ron's face that the wheels were turning.

He smirked. "I have an idea. Why don't we burn it, so we can invoke the spirits?"

"What?" Ron never fails to amaze me.

"Hey, sit your asses down and let's get this shindig going," Ron said as he grabbed a handful of the mixture and placed it in a large onyx ashtray. He lit it and joined us at the table and sat opposite Clay, while Jim sat across from me.

I waited for everyone to get settled, then said, "Put your hands on the table with your pinkies touching. We are going to ask questions and see if we can get any response through the movement of the table."

Just then, Ron Jr.'s voice came over the radio from base camp. "Okay, say something."

"Testing, one, two, three," Ron replied.

Ron Jr. replied, "Okay, sounds fine. Video's good, too."

Ready to begin, I said, "Everyone put your feet flat on the floor."

"Wait a minute, Maureen. Take a breath," Ron said.

I inhaled sharply, then exhaled.

"Oh, my God, I can see your breath."

Clay interjected. "You're right. How strange is that?"

Ron and Clay retrieved the temperature sensors and began to take the ambient temperature around the table. Clay spoke up first, "Temperature readings are in the sixties. There is no way we should see your breath, Maureen." He continued. "Ron Jr., you getting this?"

"Copy that."

I took a moment to try to get everyone to relax, using a technique I often do in meditation classes. I began, "Let's start by counting down backwards from seven, using the color of the rainbow with each number. Seven red, Six yellow, Five orange, Four blue . . ."

A low growl emanated from Jim's belly.

Collectively, the room erupted in uncontrollable laughter.

I started the countdown again.

And once again, Jim's stomach responded.

After several attempts, Jim's stomach finally remained quiet and a deathly silence enveloped the room.

———·—

I looked at Maureen, her eyes closed, her chin tucked against her chest. A low moan escaped her lips. "I feel there is someone here with us tonight." She moaned a second time, then spoke, "We would like to ask only those of white light to communicate with us. Only those whose intentions are pure and mean us no harm. Show us a sign through the table."

After a few moments, she continued, "Please. Can you show us a sign?"

Jim's voice broke the silence. "I feel the table beginning to sway."

Clay added, "Yes, there's a slight sway from me to you, Ron."

In a low whisper, Maureen moaned. "He's here." Her voice grew deeper. Her words drawn out. Through a long exhale, she said, "He sits and watches."

As the table stopped swaying, I asked, "Who are you?"

"My land," she groaned.

"Are you an Indian?"

In a deep, guttural voice, she responded, "Who asks that?"

"Just a curious one who means you no harm. Please honor me with your answer," I said.

In a deep moan, Maureen replied, "Yes and no. I am the keeper of this place." A slight laugh escaped her lips.

"Are there others with you?"

"No longer . . ."

"Do you mean the people of this house any harm?"

Maureen raised her voice, "No."

Her demeanor changed. "There's someone else here. I can feel her walking around us right now." She shifted in her chair. "The other one won't let her speak. This guy is buried here. He's old. Very old." She twisted in her chair. "He keeps trying to come in. He won't let the female speak."

"Well, if we're not getting any more response from the table, and he won't let the woman speak, why don't we just end it?"

"Okay. I'll close the circle, but I want to say a prayer."

We closed with the Our Father.

As we stood up from our chairs, Clay asked Maureen, "So who was the guy who was keeper?"

"Honest to God, he felt old, not ancient, but old." She paused. "I get the feeling he could be who he wanted to be. Ron, he's kind of like the ones that we met at Dudley Road."

We gathered our thoughts for a few minutes and decided to continue our investigation on the second floor. Ron Jr. joined us, and we all climbed to the top of stairs. I bumped into Maureen when she stopped short in front of me.

She turned and said, "The energy has shifted. It feels different." She closed her eyes and raised her hand to her brow. "I hear the name Sarah. This is bizarre. I'm getting that there is a spot around here where she used to hide."

"Do you want to try and contact her?"

Maureen looked at me and raised her eyebrows. Ignoring my question, she said, "What's that noise?"

I paused and listened. "Sounds like something is going wrong at base camp." I yelled, "Hey, guys, what's going on with base camp?"

Clay shouted from the other room, "What?"

"Listen. Do you hear that? What's going on down there?"

Before I finished my statement, Clay and Ron sprinted by me, down the stairs.

By the time we joined them, they were already fumbling with the equipment. "Monitors are all fuzzy and the audio is out." They continued, "All those cameras are in different rooms. That shouldn't happen."

I turned to look at Maureen when she entered the room. "You all right? You look a little peaked."

"I feel strange. Nauseous. Shitty, actually."

"Do you want to go outside?"

"No, I'm good. But I could use a glass of water."

Just then the static that had been abrasive to our ears was gone. The monitors returned to normal operation.

"Now that's bizarre," Ron Jr. said.

Whatever or whoever it was that was affecting the equipment isn't here now. "Still want that glass of water, Maureen? Let's go into the kitchen."

The moonlight reflected off the white tiles of the kitchen floor. "Where's the light switch?" I said as I slid my hand up and down the inside wall until I found it. "Got it."

After shuffling over to the sink, I turned on the tap. Over the sound of running water, I heard Maureen's cry. "Owwww! What the heck?!" she exclaimed, holding both hands to her head. "It . . . it . . . it hurts. So bad!"

Oh, no. How stupid of me. "This is the room where Evelyn's father killed himself."

"Thanks for telling me."

"Sorry, it didn't even dawn on me." I handed her the glass of water. "Are you okay?"

Maureen took the glass of water. Before taking a sip, she released a breath she'd been holding and then replied, "Yeah. Now that I know where the pain is coming from. It's tough to be empathic and feel how someone died."

"Do you know the story behind his death?"

"No, I don't recall."

"Evelyn's father had this catchphrase that he always used. Whenever he saw something he didn't agree with, he would say, 'Shoot the bastards.' So, one day, as a gift, his family bought him a sign that said, 'Shoot the Bastards.' He hung it in this room. Well, when he decided to end his own life, he shot himself in the head. The bullet went through his head and tore through that very sign." I picked it up from the counter and held it up for Maureen to see.

Mouth agape, she gingerly ran her finger through the bullet hole. "You know, Ron. As we always say, life *is* stranger than fiction. In this case, it truly is."

OUR THOUGHTS

MAUREEN:

As I've mentioned before, I am an open book. Eager to learn. During this investigation, the photo of the books given to us by Evelyn became one more piece to that cosmic puzzle that I mentioned earlier. It was an affirmation on how little we truly understand when it comes to how spirits can manipulate energy from the other side. My theory is that everything vibrates at different levels. For instance, a table vibrates extremely low. The particles that make up said table are packed more tightly together, making the table heavy, solid. However, what would happen if we could speed up the particles? If they were moving faster and were spread farther apart, would that same table vibrate out of existence? Hmmm? Is this what Ron and I experienced during this investigation? Sometimes investigations raise more questions than provide answers. This appears to be one of those times.

RON:

An intriguing investigation with lots of firsthand witness testimony and good physical evidence. In addition to Maureen's astute observations and the book incident, we captured audio evidence of what appears to be harpsichord music and voices by a video camera in a locked room. This one also showed me how much the history of a place can have an impact on an investigation.

Georgia

Case File: 1904876 Madison, Georgia

Location: Madison, Georgia

History: A Southern town drenched in history. Most notably known for its restored antebellum homes that were spared during Sherman's march to the sea.

Reported Paranormal Activity: None reported.

Clients: Deidre (literary agent).

Investigators: Ron (lead investigator), Maureen (trance medium).

Press: N/A.

Purpose of Investigation: To find the grave of the spirit who calls himself General Beauregard.

*T*he cool air enveloped our faces as the once colorful leaves crunched beneath our feet. As we approached the small outcropping of a building, it was as though we had been transported back in time. There was something about this house in Haverhill, Massachusetts, that immediately drew my attention. As we stepped up to the building covered with rough-hewn siding, known as the John Ward House, Ron's meter went off.

Beep beep beep.

It was him. I could feel the oh-too-familiar energy of the spirit who calls himself General Beauregard, the entity we had met so many times before.

"Ron, he's picking up where he left off before. He wants to know why you're here."

"Shit, is it my friend again?" Ron cringed. "Damn, you know he doesn't like me. I don't think this is such a good idea. I'm not in the mood for his antics."

"No kidding." Each time we've come here, it's always the same. For some reason, General Beauregard had a dislike for Ron. "He's not happy with you."

"When has he ever been? We're not even in the house and you can feel him?"

"Yeah. He's even stronger this time than last. I don't think it has anything to do with this house specifically. I just think that it reminds him of his surroundings of when he was alive."

I could feel the energy strengthen as I stepped across the threshold and stood on the old, wide-plank pine floor. A tug on the pendulum that I held in my hand confirmed it. Before I had a chance to ready myself for what was coming, a jolt of electricity traveled down my arm and into my pendulum. "Is this Nathaniel Beauregard?"

The crystal swung wildly in the small room, which was lit by the eerie light of the full moon streaming through the distorted glass in the old windows. "He says, 'Who else would it be?'"

Like a bully about to pick a fight, the spirit's energy grew agitated. I grew agitated, knowing all too well the physical altercations that had occurred in the past between Ron and me. I immediately jammed my hands, pendulum and all, into the front pockets of my jeans. The spirit's memory and mine were now the same.

Ron, watching me closely and realizing a change in my demeanor, addressed the spirit within me. "You always want respect, but you never give it in return."

The spirit's anger continued to grow.

Ron continued, "Do you have something to say, sir?"

My southern drawl sounded guttural to my own ears. "Not to the likes of you."

"It seems you annoy people in both worlds, Ron," a voice echoed in the background.

"That's funny, Jim. Did you stay up all night for that?" Ron asked.

Feeling the rage inside me building, I cried, "Ron, step back. Please."

"I'm not stepping back. I've had it with this guy."

I pleaded with Ron. I gritted my teeth as I felt the spirit's energy course through me like a shot of adrenaline. "Step back, please. I'm begging you. He wants to hurt you."

"No, I'm not afraid of him."

No longer able to restrain the spirit, I did all I could do to not pull my hands out of my pockets, but despite my best efforts, he struck out the only way he could—my body involuntarily jolted forward as I slammed into Ron repeatedly, shoving him backward against the old fieldstone fireplace.

Jim, whose jovial demeanor of a moment ago was replaced by concern, stepped in between Ron and me. "Maureen, push him out."

Jim's voice, although faint to my ears, grew louder as I regained control.

Becoming somewhat aware of my surroundings, I heard Ron's voice growing louder as he continued to address the spirit. "Is that the best you got?" he growled. "If you have something to say, say it."

A raspy voice tore from my lips. "My men! Where are my men?"

Even through the spirit's energy, I could feel the sarcasm dripping from Ron's voice. "Down south where you left them."

Because Ron had touched a nerve, the energy shifted. Instead of the anger I felt a moment ago, I was suddenly overcome with guilt. But why? Did he desert his men?

"Do you have anything else you want to say? If not, then we're done here."

As quickly as General Beauregard had arrived, his energy retreated like a wounded animal.

———

Six months later, the memory of this encounter played back in my mind as we sat in the Delta terminal at Logan airport awaiting our flight to Atlanta.

"What's on your mind, Maureen? You seem unusually quiet today."

"I was just thinking how synchronistic life can be. Six months ago, we were battling with General Beauregard. And now, we're on a road trip to find his grave."

Just then my cell phone rang. I was about to reject the call until I realized it was my sister. "Hello."

"Hi, Maureen. This is Evon."

"What's up?"

"Well, do you have a few minutes?" *I glanced at the time. One hour before take-off.* "We have time. Why? Is there something wrong?"

"I'm standing here with the girls from work, and we're about to finish moving from the Stone House to our new building." *She hesitated as if trying to find the right words.* "I don't know if you guys can do anything."

THE STONE HOUSE

Strange occurrences in a government office led its frightened manager to contact Ron, Maureen, and the New England Ghost Project. You can read all about this encounter in Episode Ten in *The Ghost Chronicles.*

The sound of clamoring voices echoed through the phone. "Everyone is a little nervous. After our encounter with the demon, we just want to make sure he doesn't follow us. I realize it's short notice, but would it be possible for you to come down here?"

"Okay. You realize we're at the airport about to board a flight to sign with our book agent."

"Oh, no. Sorry, I didn't know." Her voice quivered.

Sensing the urgency in her voice, I said, "Wait, I have an idea." I glanced at Ron as I spoke. "How about we do a remote blessing?"

"If you think it will help, we're willing!"

"Here's what I want you to do. Gather in one of the rooms and create a circle. When I tell you, I want you to repeat after me."

I could hear the sound of the ladies' shuffling feet reverberate about the empty rooms.

"We're ready."

After motioning to Ron, we stepped out of the hustle and bustle of the airport to a small alcove at the terminal. As if reading my mind, he reached into his red duffel bag and pulled out his St. Michael's prayer card.

"Okay, repeat after us: 'St. Michael, the Archangel, defend us in battle . . .'" The further into the prayer we got, the lighter the energy felt. "Evon, can you guys feel the change in energy?"

"Yes. It's like you relieved a heavy weight from our shoulders." She sighed.

Even through the phone I could sense their relief as they thanked us and said their good-byes.

Above the noise of the airport, a woman's soft voice echoed through the loud speaker. "Did you hear that? Did they just announce our flight? Come on, Ron. Let's move it. We have to go. Atlanta's a long walk."

———

After a four-hour flight and a two-hour car ride in our rented PT Cruiser, we arrived in Madison. So far, it had been a successful day. How do I measure success? Well, it was now six p.m., Ron and I had spent the whole day elbow to elbow, and I hadn't killed him yet.

"So what's that smirk for?" Ron asked.

"Who, me?" I chuckled. "Nothing. I was just thinking."

"You're always just thinking."

Ignoring Ron, I exited the car. It had already been a long day, and it was far from over. We still had to meet Deidre, our agent. After checking in to the hotel, we drove to her house.

No sooner had we arrived than we were ushered into Deidre's car and were on our way to a restaurant. Over drinks and dinner, she discussed our upcoming itinerary. Her excitement grew as we chatted and signed the contract for our new book, The Ghost Chronicles.

"You're officially authors now, and we're so happy to have you with us." Deidre looked as if she were going to burst. "I have another surprise for you." She continued, "I got permission from the Madison police for us to investigate the Madison Memorial Cemetery tonight."

"Tonight?!" Ron and I said in unison. That's the last thing we wanted to do.

"Geez. That's great, Deidre," I said, as I forced a smile on my face that I didn't quite feel.

———————

After we arrived at the cemetery, Deidre; her husband, Judd; Ron; and I pulled up next to the white-and-blue police cruiser. Two of Madison's finest—and from what Deirdre shared, the entire night shift—exited their car to greet us.

Stepping out into the warm southern night, we introduced ourselves to the officers. Although they were polite, I could sense their apprehension beneath their calm demeanor.

Deirdre turned toward Ron and me. "Where do you want to start?"

Ron looked past where we stood to the dark expanse of the cemetery and swung his arm like a conductor in mid score. "How 'bout over there?"

After walking around aimlessly for a few steps, he turned to me. "Maureen, do you have your pendulum with you?

"Yes."

"Whip it out."

"Whip it out? Excuse me."

"I want to find some spirit that can tell us where General Beauregard is located."

Above the chirping of the cicadas, I could hear the clicking of Deidre's digital camera. "Check this out! I just got an orb."

"Whoa," Judd's voice chimed in.

"It's really a big one. I have never seen one like that before. E-v-e-r!" Deidre's voice rose in glee. "Oh my, it just totally drained my battery."

"Ahhh. We always bless our equipment with holy water." I paused for a moment to gauge their response. When they didn't respond, I said, "Well, it works for us."

"Are you ready, Maureen?" Ron asked.

"Ready for what?"

"To pull 'em in. . . ."

"Don't even go there. Don't ever do that to me again," I said, even as the images of our encounter at the 1859 House surged through my mind—when his "pulling them in" nearly took me out.

"I can feel some energy, but there's no one who wants to communicate with us."

———

One look at Maureen and I could tell by her growing weariness that the events of the day were taking their toll. Impatiently, I took out my pendulum and began to dowse. As the rhodonite crystal at the end of the pendulum spun wildly, Deidre spoke up, "Ron, yours is really going."

RHODONITE

A pink to red manganese silicate mineral used in the metaphysical realm to aid in discovering and developing hidden talents, compassion, love, and generosity. Its name is derived from a Greek word meaning "rose-red."

Asking the pendulum, I said, "I need some help. I'm looking for Nathaniel Beauregard. Is Nathaniel Beauregard here in this part of the cemetery?"

No.

"Can you show me where Nathaniel Beauregard or his family is located?"

The pendulum pointed toward our right, indicating the location where we should go. "Oh, yeah!" Following the response from the pendulum, I gestured the group to follow me deeper into the cemetery.

After a few minutes of sidestepping the stones, I looked to Maureen, who had her hand to her forehead. "Are you getting anything?"

"I feel something. The pressure is intensifying on the left side of my head. I think it's around here. You know, Ron, there's a lot of energy around us. It's interesting. I can sense them. It's as if the spirits here are pacing back and forth. It just feels strange to me."

Once again, I paused and began to dowse. "Is Nathaniel Beauregard or his family in this section of the cemetery?"

No.

"Crap. Is there anyone who wants to speak with us?"

No.

"Well, we didn't just come a thousand miles not to find this guy. I'm going to check out over there," I said as I pointed my flashlight to a grouping of what appeared to be older tombstones.

I studied the graves for a moment, then called out to the rest of the group. "A lot of these graves are marked unknown."

Deidre spoke up, "Yes, that's what I find so haunting."

As the beam of light shone on the stone, I read them out loud. "Mississippi cavalry. Tennessee infantry." I paused for a moment to reflect. "It is so sad that they are buried here and not at home."

"As a matter of fact, we're not far from the field hospital. It's just right over there." Deidre pointed past the grove of pecan trees that lined a nearby railroad track. While I half-listened to what she was telling me, my meter began to beep. At first it was low, but grew louder and louder with each step I took toward the railroad track. "Maureen, come 'ere. Quick."

"Oooh, yeah. I can feel the energy. It's intense," Maureen said as she came up from behind me.

One of the two officers, who had been hanging back, stepped forward. "Do you think you've found him?"

"That's what I'm trying to find out." I thought for a moment, then asked, "Are there any wires or electricity here?"

He spoke up with a southern drawl. "No. None that I know of. What is that you're using?"

"It's a cell sensor. An electromagnetic field meter. Do you remember when they had the brain cancer scare from cell phones?"

"Yes."

"They invented these to test for high EMF. One of the theories used by paranormal investigators is that there is a correlation between EMF and paranormal activity. When we do an investigation, we usually walk through the place and measure sources of radiation. There are naturally occurring sources like wiring, TVs, radios, microwaves, and clock radios, to name a few."

The blare of the meter slowed to a crawl. I took a step forward. The meter beeped loudly. I took another step. It beeped again. "It seems like the energy is moving."

Maureen chimed in, "I told you they're moving all around us. Looks like they're leading you."

"Look, over here. There's more CSA [Confederate States of America] graves," I said as I shined the light across the moss-covered slate stones." As I went from stone to stone, "Unknown.

Unknown. They are all unknown. This makes our job harder. Nathaniel Beauregard could be buried here, and we wouldn't even know it. Maureen, why don't you try dowsing here?"

"Okay," she replied as she raised her pendulum. "Is there anyone here?"

Yes.

Through a series of questions and answers, we were able to determine that we had connected with an infantry soldier from Georgia who fought for the CSA. I spoke up, "We need your help. We're looking for any Beauregards buried here in this cemetery. Do you know of any?" *The last question sounded desperate, even to my own ears.*

Maureen replied, "I don't think they know. Just because someone is buried here doesn't mean they're aware of everyone who is buried here."

Still not completely satisfied, I continued, "Do you have anything else to say?"

No.

"Okay. Thank you."

I glanced at one of the officers who now seemed to be intently watching us and took the opportunity to address him. "Do you know what she was doing?"

"Kind of. Deidre was telling me a little bit about it before."

"Did you ever hear about dowsing for water?"

"I can't say that I have. Wait. Is that with a willow branch?"

"Yup, that's it. Up north, the utility companies use L-shaped rods to find lines and water. Out west, oil companies use them. In fact, during the Vietnam war, the Army used dowsers to find Viet Cong tunnels. It is an old method, and I didn't believe in it myself until I started using it. What she was doing is using the pendulum to do spiritual dowsing."

"Yeah, that was very interesting."

"We use other stuff, like this thermometer," I said as I grabbed the black teardrop-shaped instrument on a lanyard around my neck. "If someone tells us they feel a cold spot, we can actually measure it. We use digital recorders, infrared cameras, thermal imaging, and other pieces of equipment as well."

Deidre, who had been standing beside us patiently listening, interjected, "This section we're in now always seems cold no matter what time of the day it is."

Thermometer still in my hand, I pressed the button. "Yes, it actually is. Look at the reading."

"Wow! That's crazy," the officer exclaimed. He pivoted his stance. "Hey, on the other side over there are the graves of two police officers who died in the line of duty. Would you mind looking at their graves for me?"

"Sure," I replied.

"It's quite a ways." He pointed off into the darkness. "They are all the way over there by the tree line."

"It's okay. If you don't mind walking, I don't mind. That is the least we can do for you taking your time to accompany us here. Can you show us where they are?"

"Yes, follow me."

Raising my voice, I addressed the group, "Okay, everyone, we are moving to a new location."

"Thank you. The last thing I want to do is to take you away from what you were doing," the officer said.

"That's all right. Things happen for a reason, and if this is important enough for you to ask, then we are more than willing to help."

Maureen stepped up to my side. "Where are we going, Ron?"

"We're heading over to the other side of the cemetery to look at a couple of graves for this officer."

"Oh, all right."

While we walked down and over the uneven tufts of grass, I asked the officer, "Why do you want us to look at these graves in particular?"

"Well, these two officers have been kind of forgotten. In fact, we just found out about one of them recently. We heard from Deidre about what you do, and after observing you tonight, it seemed like the right thing to do."

As we reached the top of the hill, the officer stopped. "Here's the first one."

Flashlight in hand, I bent over to read the epitaph. "This is MacAdams. Percy MacAdams." Curious, I asked the officer, "So why are they buried in this part of the cemetery?"

"Sorry. I don't know."

I took a closer look at the stone. "Looks like he died in 1931."

"My heart is racing," Maureen said as she clutched her chest.

"He was breaking up a fight and somebody shot him."

Maureen continued, "I feel like his heart was rushing when he died."

"That makes sense. He probably would have had an adrenalin rush."

"Were they killed at the same time?" I spoke up.

"No. They died at different times in separate incidents."

Judd, who had moved in closer to read the stone, said, "Looks like he was thirty-two when he died."

"Okay. Let's see if we can make contact. Percy MacAdams, are you with us now?" I asked via pendulum again.

No.

"Really. He's not here?"

"That's good. That means he's passed on to a happy place where he is supposed to be," Deidre intoned.

"That makes sense."

"Did the other one die earlier or later?"

"Later."

"Where is he buried?" I asked.

"Way over there." The officer pointed off into the distance again. "It will take a little bit to find him."

Within minutes, we were standing by the grave.

I flashed the light on the granite and read, "Fred Adams. Looks like he died in 1945. I believe that's during the war?"

Maureen, who had been relatively quiet for the past half hour, which was extremely unusual, screeched, "Ow! What the heck? I am getting a pain in my stomach." She gritted her teeth and groaned. "It's burning."

I stepped back toward Maureen and placed my hand on her shoulder to comfort her. Through her obvious pain, she spoke up, "How was he killed?"

"He was shot by a restaurant owner in Madison without provocation. He was on patrol, and the restaurant owner hailed him over to the curb. He drove over to the man, and before he could even get out of the car, he shot him."

"So, basically, it was an assassination?" I said.

"Basically."

"Oh, my God." Maureen got louder. "The pain. It burns."

"Wow. That's interesting," the officer intoned. "That's what it feels like when you get shot."

"Maureen, why don't we try to communicate?"

She inhaled deeply and then exhaled. "Give me a minute, please."

We stood in silence listening to the loud chirping of cicadas as we waited for Maureen to regain her composure.

After what seemed like an eternity, but couldn't have been more than a minute or two, Maureen spoke up, "I'm ready." Grasping the crystal pendulum, she began, "Fred, are you here?"

Yes.

As Maureen continued with the pendulum, we discovered that Fred knew who had killed him but never understood why.

"He wants you to know that he's thankful to the two of you for bringing us here and giving him a voice. You are family. Brothers in blue."

The officers glanced at each other, then turned back to us, with looks of satisfaction.

I spoke up, "Fred, we want to let you know that you and Mac-Adams will not be forgotten. We will make people aware that you died in the line of duty. I promise."

Maureen continued, "Fred, anything else you want to say?"

The spirit spoke through her, "Watch your back."

"What? Watch my back?" one of the officers asked nervously.

Maureen corrected him. "No, he's saying that Ron should watch his back."

"Duly noted. Thank you, Fred." I chuckled. "Looks like I have another member in my posse on the other side." Exhaustion creeping in, I said, "So I think we should call it a night. I honestly don't think we're going to find this Beauregard character."

"Ron, can I talk to you for a minute?" one of the officers said as he placed his hand on my shoulder. "I'd like to speak with you and Maureen alone, if you don't mind."

"Sure. What's up?"

His eyes darted from the ground to my own as he seemed to wait for everyone to be out of earshot. Deidre's voice rang out in the darkness, "You guys coming?"

"Go ahead. We'll be there in a minute."

I turned back to the officer who was jingling the keys in his pocket. "Okay. What's up?"

"I'd like to talk to you about a case that I'm working on. It's kind of personal in nature. Are you available at any time during the next couple of days?"

"Sure. We'll be here through the weekend."

"If you don't mind, that would be great. My shift doesn't start until late tomorrow. How about tomorrow morning?"

"Sure. Why don't we meet at Deidre's. Say around eleven a.m.?"

"That works for me. See you then."

———·—·———

The next morning, I spoke to Deidre in her parlor. "I hope you don't mind, but we invited one of the officers to join us here for a few minutes."

"Not at all. I was wondering what that was all about. When's he coming?"

"About now." I chuckled as the doorbell rang. *Timing is everything,* I thought.

Judd poked his head into the parlor and said, "Ron and Maureen, you've got a visitor."

We took a moment to exchange pleasantries, and then I said, "Deidre, is there someplace more private where we can talk with this gentleman?"

"Sure, why don't you two take him upstairs. There's a little office off to the right that you can use."

My mind raced, I found myself, getting more curious by the minute. *What does he really want from us?*

We squeezed into the small office and closed the door behind us.

The officer began. "Do you remember I told you last night that I'm working on this case. Well, it's an automobile crash that has been ruled an accident." He paused, then said, "But I think it's more than that. There's something about it that just doesn't sit right. And I'm hoping you can help."

"Well, what are you looking for?"

He withdrew a pack of photographs from his pocket and waved them before us. "I think one of these people is involved," he said as he placed several photographs one by one on the table before us. "Can you tell me if you think I'm on the right track, Maureen?"

———·—·———

"Sure. Give me a moment," I said. My stomach clenched as I thought about the huge responsibility of what I was doing. Reading for people is difficult sometimes, but this . . . this carries with it a whole other level of importance. I picked up the photographs and inspected them one by one. Each picture held varying levels of energy. I closed my eyes to focus my intentions and found it difficult as the room suddenly grew smaller. The atmosphere changed as I felt the added weight of the officer's nervous anticipation.

Once again I glanced at the photographs. I reached out to the one that had held the strongest energy. As I grasped it between my thumb and forefinger, a vision suddenly flashed before my mind. "I see a truck hitting a tree. I think this guy might have something to do with it."

The officer's eyes grew wider, as he replied, "Can you expand on that?"

"I think the brake line was tampered with."

He raised his voice. "Are you sure about that?"

My stomach clenched even tighter, if that was even possible. "I believe so. But let's try something a little different, just to be sure." I thought for a moment, then said, "I'd like for you to take a piece of paper and write down the names of those you believe are involved, as well as some fictitious names. Be sure to leave enough space between them so that I can rip it into pieces."

The officer whipped his note pad out of his pocket. "I can do that. Just give me a sec."

When he finished, he handed me the piece of paper. I carefully tore the sheet into strips, one name on each piece. "Ron, can you fold these up so the name is not visible."

Before me lay a half dozen of folded-up pieces of paper. I spread them out in an even line on the table.

I reached into my pocket and pulled out my crystal pendulum.

"So what are you going to do?" the officer asked.

"Do you remember when we dowsed last night in the cemetery?"

"Of course, I do. It was pretty interesting."

"Okay, well, in order to make sure I'm not influencing the results, we're going to do a blind test. The trick is to be specific with our question so as to not leave room for error. Okay. Here we go." I raised the pendulum and lined it up to the far left of the names. Then I asked, "Can you please point me in the direction of the person who was involved with the accident that this officer is investigating?"

I continued to move the pendulum from left right, hesitating on each folded piece of paper, to see if I received a response. As I approached the middle of the line, the pendulum began to swing counterclockwise, indicating a yes. I continued moving over the remaining papers with no response. I grasped the pendulum tighter and placed it over the paper that it had reacted to earlier and repeated my question.

The pendulum swung wildly. "I think we got our answer. It's definitely a yes."

Like a kid at Christmas, the officer quickly unfolded the paper and read the name. An involuntary gasp escaped his lips. "I don't know how you did this, but this is the name of the person whose photograph you picked out earlier." He paused, then slammed his open palm down on the table. "I knew it. This was the guy I thought was involved all along. I just need to find a way to prove it." The officer gathered up the photographs, stuffed them back into the manila envelope, and shook our hands. "I can't thank you both enough. I really appreciate this."

"No problem. Glad we could help."

————

As we stood in the security line at the Atlanta airport, thoughts of the whirlwind weekend coursed through my mind. I was amazed that we were able to cram so much into so little time. We investigated not only the cemetery but also Deidre's house, the Heritage house, the restaurant, and the Rose cottage as well. Not to mention the case we worked on. All in all, it was fun, but right now, all I wanted was to sleep in my own bed.

The sound of the TSA agent speaking pulled me out of my day-dream. "Sir, can you step this way, please?"

Ron was escorted to the side of the belt where he was approached by a formidable-looking female agent. *Oh boy, now what? I thought* as the agent held up a clear plastic suitcase liner bag filled with equipment. "What's this stuff, sir?"

Ron flashed a nervous grin as he spoke. "That's my ghost-hunting equipment. I'm a paranormal investigator."

"Really?"

"Yes, if you'd like to see it, I even have a newspaper article with me on the investigation we just completed in Madison."

Like turning on a light switch, her face lit up. "Wow, you're not going to believe this, or maybe you will." She laughed. "I have a ghost in my house, you know."

Ron looked at me with a here-we-go-again expression on his face. "That's interesting."

"Yeah, let me tell you all about it." Barely even taking a breath, she continued, "Bertha, as I like to call her, takes real good care of me. It started with little things, like shutting off the lights when I leave them on. Now, she tidies my house for me: she makes my bed, vacuums the rug, and even dusts."

"How come we can't find any like that?" *I chuckled.*

"Oh, yes. All my friends think it's so cool, I— "

Just then I noticed the clock on the wall behind her. "Sorry to interrupt, but our flight is boarding now. Can we leave?"

"Sure. But if you guys are ever out this way again, I'd love to have you investigate my house."

"We'd be happy to. Here's my card. Send me an email when you have a chance."

She tucked the card into her pocket. Ron quickly stuffed his equipment into his carry-on, and we headed toward the gate. *I thought to myself, Seems this joy ride will never end.*

OUR THOUGHTS

MAUREEN:

There have been times during my medium/psychic career when I've come to the realization that I needed to choose my words wisely, moments when I could feel the weight of responsibility that was placed upon my shoulders. Our time with this officer certainly was one of those defining moments. And although it gave me pause, I honestly feel that the information we provided, if nothing else, helped to confirm his own suspicions and just maybe could help him on the path to find the physical proof he so desperately needed to bring justice to the victim.

RON:

A whirlwind weekend of investigating. It started in a house in Haverhill, Massachusetts, and ended in a cemetery in Madison, Georgia. Although we didn't find the results we were looking for, we were able to help several people along the way, including being able to put to rest the minds of the workers at the Stone House, helping the police in Georgia, and giving several building owners clues as to who and why their places are haunted. We even found time to listen to a TSA worker share her story.

New London Ledge Lighthouse

Case File: 194987 New London Ledge Lighthouse

Location: New London, Connecticut

History: Built in 1909 on the Southwest Ledge; the Coast Guard took over in 1939, and the light was automated in 1987. The legend: The wife of Ernie, the lighthouse keeper, ran off with the captain of the Block Island Ferry. In his despair, Ernie jumped from the roof of the lighthouse to his death.

Reported Paranormal Activity: Unexplained knockings at night, doors opening and closing repeatedly, television and lights turning on and off, and sheets being pulled off beds. The voice of a woman whispering can be heard above the sound of the wind.

Clients: *American Builders* television show: Brian Gurry (host, construction worker), Jimmy Lemire (host), Mark Apostolon (producer).

Investigators: Ron (lead investigator), Maureen (trance medium), Ron Jr. (investigator), Jim (photographer), Karen (EVP specialist), Jeremy D'Entremont (lighthouse historian).

Purpose of Investigation: To give Jimmy, *American Builder* star, the experience of a real paranormal investigation while being filmed for the show.

Length of Investigation: Overnight stay at New London Ledge Lighthouse.

*T*he phone rang, shattering my concentration. Grabbing the receiver, I glanced at the caller ID. Now what? "Hey, Ron."

"We did it! American Builder *won an Emmy.*"

"Get outta here."

"Seriously. Mark just called me." He paused. "Have you even watched it yet?"

Inwardly, I groaned. "You know I don't like watching myself."

"Get over it. How can you not watch it? Everybody else has seen it." Ron chuckled.

Funny. "Whatever. I'll watch it when I have time." Done with this conversation, I dumped him. "Look, I gotta go."

"Fine. Call me later."

With our conversation still hanging in the air, I pressed the end button and dropped the phone in the base.

With Ron's words grating on my conscience, a battle ensued between my reluctance to watch myself channeling and my curiosity. Curiosity won.

With a sigh, I dragged myself over to the entertainment center and opened the drawer. The colorful DVD caught my attention. Even as my heart began to beat wildly in my chest, I reached for it.

I can't bear to watch myself channel.

Seeing someone else's essence inhabit my body is disturbing, even to me.

The house was empty. If I was ever going to watch the show, now was the time. I shoved the DVD in the player, reluctantly plopped myself on the couch, and began to watch.

Halfway through the episode, I heard a car door slam. Pausing the video, I walked into my kitchen to greet my unknown visitor. Oh, great, it was my mother.

"Hi, honey. What are you up to?"

"Not much." Oooh, not now. I suddenly felt like a child caught in a lie.

As if she sensed I was hiding something, she walked past me and into the living room. She hesitated for only a moment before stepping in front of the television, where my frozen image lit up the screen. "Isn't that you?" She paused. "That can't be the DVD I've been waiting months for, is it?" She looked at me, eyes narrowing, lips pursing.

Unable to lie to my mother. As if I could. "Yeah. It's the American Builder *show we were on. Ron just told me it won an Emmy."*

"Oooh, great. Can we watch it?" Without a response, she removed her jacket, tossed it on the arm of the couch, and sat down with a whoosh. She patted the cushion beside her. "Come on, sit down. We can watch it together."

I felt my stomach drop to my toes. This was the last thing I really wanted to do.

"Back it up a bit. I want to see it all."

In an attempt to delay the inevitable, I quipped, "You sure? It's really long."

She turned her head slowly, giving me "the look." After forty years, I could not deny what that meant. "Fine." I hit play.

Within moments, the dreaded scene arrived. I heard my voice emanating from the television. "It's a warning." If memory served, the horror of the moment was about to be revealed. With one eye on my mother and the other on the television, I watched as her enthusiasm waned. The sound of my screams echoed through the speakers. The moment I had been avoiding had arrived.

My mother's body stiffened. Unable to take her eyes away from the screen, she gently laid her frail hand on my lap. She sensed my discomfort and gently squeezed my thigh. We sat in an awkward silence for what seemed like an eternity until the video was over. I held my breath while she collected her thoughts.

Just as I was about to stand, she turned. Staring at me through unshed tears, she said, "Are you okay? Should you be doing this?" Her voice quivered. "I'm scared for you."

"I'm okay, Mom. Trust me."

But was I really? I began to doubt myself as the events of a few months earlier began to flash in my mind, as if they were happening now. Ron standing on the lower deck of the ship, his raspy voice bellowing above the motor.

"Be careful with that shit, will you?!" I bellowed, as I watched Ron Jr. and Maureen loading the equipment on the boat. Before I had a chance to collect my thoughts, a burly man in a red baseball cap, cargo shorts, and a cut-off tee landed on the deck with a thump.

Tattooed arms and muscles to spare, Jimmy extended his hand. "How you doing, buddy?" My fingers pulsed beneath his grasp. *Geez, what a grip!*

So focused on Jimmy coming aboard, I barely noticed the cameraman hovering around us. The blinking red light on the top of his camera drew my attention. I quickly realized the camera was rolling. I shifted my stance and grabbed the side of the fish well that stood between Jimmy and me. In an attempt to intimidate the hulk that stood in front of me, I quipped, "We're here to scare the heck out of you."

As if searching for an answer, Jimmy began to rub the palms of his hands together. "I'm a big-time—"

I completed his sentence. "Non-believer, right?"

"Yeah. Totally. I'm a big-time non-believer. You'll never make a believer out of me," he spat out as he continued to fidget from one foot the other, his hands moving continuously.

His words said one thing; his body language said another. *Maybe he isn't as tough as I thought he was.* I continued, "You're used to physical things. Things you can pick up."

"Yeah. Things you can pick up and throw." He added, "Show me what you got."

"Hope you brought some extra underwear."

My response went unanswered. *It was going to be an interesting night.*

The deck bobbed beneath our feet as Jimmy and I completed the interview on the bow of the ship. The deep groan of the foghorn made me realize we were almost there. I glanced up to the red-and-white brick structure growing larger on the horizon. Within moments, the ship scraped up against the mammoth concrete island protruding from the ocean. With the boat tied off, we began hoisting our equipment up the long ladder to the base of the lighthouse. As the last piece of equipment came up the ladder, Jimmy stood by the rail. "Bye-bye, boat," he said, as our only form of transportation departed for the night. While the team assembled base camp, I watched as Jimmy was being filmed for the show. He grabbed the door of the Porta-Potty. "They tell me this is the most haunted lighthouse. I made a sled out of these once." He paused. "If I ever get in trouble, I know I can make a boat out of this."

One of the production staff hurried to Jimmy's side and began fidgeting with the wireless mic receiver on his belt. "I'm getting clicks."

I chimed in, "Could be paranormal, you know. You may want to listen to them later. You might even catch an EVP."

"It's probably low batteries," Jimmy said as he adjusted his stance to allow for easier access to the device.

After the mic was repaired, we began our tour of the lighthouse. From the basement, we quickly moved to the recently repaired first floor. There Maureen stopped short.

Jimmy said, "Maureen, you're looking uncomfortable."

"I'm feeling a lot of energy right now. Pain in my head. My chest. I'm getting a sense that they want to show themselves tonight."

"Whatever. Let's move on," I said. Stairs creaking beneath our feet, we made our way to the second floor. We walked past strewn lumber and peeling plaster, entering the first room on the left. Base camp.

Jimmy stepped over to Ron Jr., who was sitting in front of the monitors. "Okay, who do we have here? And what's he doing?"

"We set these up throughout the building," Ron Jr. remarked as he held the thermometer up for the camera. "If there's a sudden drop in temperature, it'll register here." He continued, "And these are the monitors to the infrared camera that gives us the ability to see remotely what's going on in low light."

"Okay, let's move on," I said, exiting the room. I looked over my shoulder to Jimmy and Maureen, who were trailing close behind. "Next stop, the lamp room."

Hand over hand, I climbed up the iron ladder, through the narrow opening in the floor of the lamp room. I squinted because of the bright sun as I stepped aside to make room for Maureen and Jimmy. The small, bright space was a stark contrast to the dimly lit rooms below. As we adjusted to the confines of the space, Jimmy and I chatted about the upcoming events. I stopped in mid-sentence as Maureen's lack of movement caught my attention. I studied her for a moment. Although she seemed to be looking out to sea, her mind seemed to be somewhere else. An all-too-familiar look crossed her face.

"We have company up here," I said.

————

I didn't need Ron to tell me what I already knew. "Yes," I murmured.

Jimmy stepped closer to me. "Maureen, are they following us around?"

Unable to respond, I stood transfixed. I stared at Jimmy's reflection mirrored in the lens of the lamp as I struggled to maintain control. While my consciousness ebbed and flowed between the here and the hereafter, my survival instincts kicked in. Small space. Open floor. Narrow ladder. Not the ideal place to allow a spirit to share my body. As I fought off the urge to channel, I said, "I think we need to go down now."

As if sensing my dilemma, Ron reached out and grabbed me by the elbow. "Okay, now's not a good time. Let's go. Down, down, down."

Jimmy descended the ladder first. My turn. My stomach suddenly clenched in knots, I struggled to regain my focus. Assuring that my foot was carefully planted on each rung of the ladder, I gingerly made my descent to the floor below.

"I think we ought to check out the basement before it gets too late." Ron gestured to Jimmy and me.

"Do we have to?" Jimmy replied with a nervous stutter. "I tried to go down by myself earlier. I took a couple steps and by the third step I felt a buzz and thought not by myself."

Ignoring Jimmy's babbling, the stairs creaked beneath our feet as we descended into the dank basement of the lighthouse. Although the atmosphere grated on my nerves, whatever had been reaching out earlier in the lamp room felt more distant, as if the energy blended into the background. But something told me that tonight was going to be a totally different story. "Not really getting anything to speak of." Not waiting for Ron to respond, I started back up the stairs.

As darkness engulfed the lighthouse, Ron announced, "Let's try an EVP experiment in the children's room first."

Once we ascended the stairs to the third floor and entered the children's room, the air felt charged, different from the first floor. Within a few moments, Ron, Karen, Jimmy, and I placed the folding chairs in a circle around a lit candelabra, the only light in the room.

The shadow of Mark and the cameraman grew larger as they made their way closer to the circle.

"This is the room where the Japanese camera crew supposedly had their equipment thrown at them. They were found cowering in the corner, in the alcoves of the room," Ron explained.

I couldn't help but notice Jimmy's smirk. A part of me—maybe I should feel bad—wanted nothing more than to have him experience something that would wipe that smirk off his face.

Mark interrupted, "Hey, did someone say, 'Get out of my face'?"

Collectively, we responded, "No, we didn't hear anything."

"I heard it in my earpiece."

"Oh, my God. That's the kind of evidence that I want," Karen replied as she began babbling about residual energy.

I turned to stare at Jimmy, who had his eyes closed, seeming unimpressed.

Ron, always the comedian, began to wave his hand up and down in front of Jimmy's face. "You asleep?"

"Just resting my eyes."

Karen picked up where she left off, once again babbling about residual energy.

Thud.

In unison, we jerked in our seats and glared into the dimly lit recesses of the room.

Karen chimed in. "See, there you go. They're starting already." She continued, "This is the children's room. Maybe there are children here, and they are playing games with us?"

The sudden pressure in my left temple coincided with Karen's words. As it began to throb, I instinctively pressed my hand against the side of my head in an attempt to lessen the pain. "No, they are here. It feels different."

Jimmy's words came through, along with his shit-eating grin. "Yeah, right!"

He just didn't get it. At moments like this, I just wanted to pop him one.

"Let's try to capture an EVP now," Karen said as she turned on the two digital recorders in her hands. "Ready to record," she said, "Could you give us a message, please?"

Words echoed in my mind. "I'm hearing someone say something about the big man." I paused for moment. "They don't like the big man."

Jimmy piped up, still wearing his arrogant grin. He began flexing his muscles and chuckling. "They don't want no part of the J-Rock."

Yeah, that's what I'm thinking.

"You got it," Ron quipped.

Karen, ignoring the banter, continued, "Let's just try this again."

The shift in energy grew stronger. "You're dealing with something different now. It's not the same," I said.

Once again, my words fell on deaf ears, as Karen continued, "Spirits, speak to us, please. Are you here? Yes or no."

We waited, hearing nothing but the whirring sound of her recorder. Moments felt like hours as we quietly waited for a reply.

"Okay, let's see if we got anything." Karen rewound the recorders and hit play.

Her voice crackled through the recorder. "Spirits, speak to us, please. Are you here? Yes or no."

A hiss erupted out of static, "Yesss."

Immediately, I looked for Jimmy's reaction. Eyes once closed and relaxed were now wide open. His gaze shifting left to right. His smug smile no longer visible.

Good.

Jimmy stuttered. "Tell me . . ." He cleared his throat. "Tell me," he hesitated, as if struggling for the right words, "Didn't something just answer you back?"

Karen's posture stiffened, as a smug smile crossed her lips. "We caught something."

"Replay that," Jimmy commanded.

"Yesss."

Much to his disbelief, we all heard the same "yes" response to Karen's question over and over again. For a brief second, I could have sworn I saw fear in his eyes. But it left as soon as it came.

"That was cool," Ron interjected. "Why don't we take a break for a bit and then we'll see what else we can stir up."

The "oh shit" look on Jimmy's face was priceless. But unlike Jimmy, I found myself eagerly anticipating the events to come.

Our bodies draped haphazardly over the wooden benches of the safe room. Just as we were getting comfortable, Ron, with his irritating voice, bellowed, "Back to work. The night's gettin' short." Turning abruptly, he looked about the room. "Hey, where's Karen?"

No sooner had the words left Ron's lips than the outside door swooshed open. Karen and the J-Rock rushed in.

"Where the hell were you guys?" Ron spat.

As is typical, Karen dismissed Ron's words. "Hey, guys, guess what we got?!"

"Let me guess. An EVP," Ron said.

"The previous paranormal group photographed an apparition by the outside stairs of the lighthouse. So Jimmy and I did an EVP session there."

"And . . ."

"Well, we got a Class A EVP saying, 'Help me. I'm cold.'"

"Of course, you did."

"What's the plan?" Mark asked as he rose to his feet.

"Why don't we go back to the third floor and do a Ouija board session?"

The cameraman chimed in, "Ouija board?"

"Yeah, why not?" Ron chuckled as he held up the glow-in-the-dark planchette. "It's not like Maureen's head is gonna spin around and she'll start puking pea soup."

"Ha-ha-ha. Funny, Ron." *I wished I could be as confident.*

Sitting cross-legged on the dusty hardwood floor, Ron placed the Ouija board in the center of the group. He lit the candelabra and placed it to my right. Next, he positioned the infrared camera on the floor, maneuvering the lens to encompass the board. Radio in hand, he said, "Ron Jr., how's the video feed? You getting this?"

Ron Jr.'s voice crackled through the speaker. "Yup. Looks good."

Turning toward the camera crew that were huddling with their backs toward the wall, Ron asked, "You guys ready?"

Mark gave Ron the thumbs up.

"Maureen, you all set?"

I nodded a yes in response.

Anticipation began to set in as I scanned the room. Ron placed the planchette on the board. Karen sat across from me, her recorder placed between Jimmy and her.

"Let's go," *Ron said.* "Ouija board experiment, 12:45 a.m."

We lightly placed our fingertips on the glowing planchette. Within seconds of Ron speaking, it carried our fingers across the board, moving in a circular motion.

"Boooooo!" *Jimmy mocked.*

Abruptly, it changed direction, then stopped. Through the looking glass of the planchette, the letter U appeared. Without hesitating, it slid over the next letter.

"G?"

Ron leaned in for a better look. "G. Yeah, that's a G."

The planchette picked up the pace and slid back and forth across the board.

"Oh, look. Now it's an O," *Karen stammered.* "What? What are you trying to tell us?"

"U. G. O."

Once again, the planchette's rhythm picked up as it ricocheted between the G and the O. Over and over again.

"*Do you want us to leave this place?*" *Ron asked, responding to the board.* "*Are you trying to tell us something? Do you want us to go?*"

"*Go,*" *Karen sputtered this time.* "*Go, go. You want us to go? We can't go. Where can we go? We were left here,*" *Karen's voice escalated.* "*Who are you?*"

Before the last of her words left her mouth, the planchette stopped dead.

For a moment, we sat in silence.

I knew what we had to do next. "*Let's hold hands.*"

"*Fine, whatever,*" *Ron spat out as we all joined hands to amplify the connection.*

It worked.

Once again, we asked the question, "*Do you want us to go?*"

The air shifted. With it, my third eye tingled.

Out of nowhere, thoughts, feelings not of my own, invaded my mind. "*I think it's a warning.*"

"*A warning?*" *Ron asked.*

"*Yeah. A warning. Like a—*"

"*Crrrrrkkkkk, crrrrrkk,*" *a crackle of static flooded the room.*

"*The video feed's gone,*" *Ron Jr.'s voice echoed through the radio.* "*We lost the monitors. The temperature's dropping.*"

Jimmy's face was suddenly ashen through the flickering flame of the candelabra. His piercing eyes darted about the room as he searched in vain for the source of the disturbance. The crackling sound of the monitors grew louder and louder.

Maureen shifted. My hand pulsated as she tightened her grip.

Her head down, swaying from side to side, she whispered, "Why are you here?"

I tossed the question back to Maureen. "Why are we here?"

Like a game of chess, she replied, "Why are you here?"

I continued, "Do you like us being here?"

"No." She raised her head, making eye contact with me, and said, "You are interfering. Please leave. Now."

Not knowing what to say, frustration growing, I blurted out, "Do you know you're dead? It's time for you to go."

Whatever entity Maureen was channeling chose to ignore my question. Instead, she said, "There's someone else here."

Her voice was soft, distant. She said, "Angry." She raised her head yet again and gazed into my eyes. That's when I knew we were in trouble.

"Ooh, we've got a new visitor. There's someone else here," I declared. "Who is here with us?"

A growl emanated deep from within her. Teeth gritted. Eyes full of hate. Whoever it was that was lingering in the darkness had arrived.

"You lie!" she bellowed. "You lie."

Maureen inhaled sharply. Her attention shifted from me. As if her head grew heavy, it dropped.

Her voice changed. It softened. "So angry."

She continued, "They left me," as if she was reliving a painful moment.

"Where?" I asked.

"Outside," she whispered. "On top of the . . ."

I completed her sentence. "Are you on the roof of the lighthouse?"

"Yes . . . down." She cried. Her fingers grew tighter, crushing mine, like a death grip.

"They left you on the roof of the lighthouse?" I asked.

"Yes. Down. Get down." She screeched, agitation growing.

"They left you?"

Maureen's body stiffened. Slowly, she raised her head. Once again I was gazing in those oh-too-familiar eyes—eyes that could tear a hole through your soul.

"Is she all right?" Jimmy piped in.

"Yeah, she's fine."

Just then, breaking her grip, she grabbed her head, crying out in agony.

Concerned for her health, I knew I had to break the connection the spirit had on her.

"Maureen. Maureen, push him out," I said in an attempt to bring her back to us. I took a step forward. "Maureen, push him out."

Even as I advanced, she dug the heels of her shoes into the floor and shoved her body backward, farther away.

Now on my knees, I grabbed her shoulders. Without hesitation, she repelled my advance and shoved me backward into the lit candelabra.

Regaining my balance, I pushed back and strengthened my grip on her shoulders. "Push him out, Maureen."

After she heard my words, her body slackened, grew limp. Once again, she clutched her head, her breathing labored. "My head. Ow, my head! It feels like it's been split wide open."

"It probably was." I gathered my thoughts. "That's interesting. It's kind of like the story, but different."

"Should we go downstairs now?" the cameraman man spoke up.

"Give me a minute," Maureen responded as she continued to bring her breathing back to normal.

Karen quipped, "Hey, Jimmy, I saw your fingers turning purple."

"My hand was tingling. That's how much pressure she had on my hand."

"Yeah, she has a grip on her."

He chuckled. "Yeah, I'm not gonna be a sissy and say, 'Oh, let go of my hand.'" Jimmy started to walk away, then stopped and turned. "The last time I felt that much pressure on my hand, my wife was pushing my daughter out." He finished his words, shaking his head; then he descended the stairs down to the first floor.

Exhausted, we sat in the safe room, contemplating what we had just experienced. "Hey Ron," Mark spoke up. "What did you mean when you said, 'It's kind of like the story but different'?"

"Well, you know the story about Ernie, don't you?"

"Kind of."

Jeremy, eager to respond said, "It's possible the spirit that Maureen channeled is the spirit of Ernie that the legend is based on. Basically, the story's all there. A worker got locked out on the roof, tried to get down, and instead fell to his death. For an accident to a laborer, well, that might not have made the newspapers. It might have been kept quiet at the time."

Mark added, "It only makes sense. All urban legends have their roots in truth. This could be the case with the legend of Ernie."

"I don't know about you guys, but I'm so tired, I can't think anymore. Why don't we try to catch some Zzzzs?"

Moments later, when I was curled up on a lawn chair, my head grew heavy, my breathing shallow, as the chaos of the day became nothing but a memory. The much-needed rest was now at hand.

"Ohhhh-wahhhh, ohhhh-wahhh, ohhhh-wahhhhh." The foghorn blew.

Jumping to my feet, I stumbled, righting myself. I knocked over the chair.

Great. *This is gonna be a long night.*

After sparring with the foghorn all night, sunrise came way too soon. The boat finally arrived to rescue us from this nightmare.

Pleased that we had once again managed to pull it off, to provide a client with an experience to remember, we quickly packed our gear. No sooner than we had, with a tight schedule to keep, we were on board watching the lighthouse disappear into the fog.

I turned toward Jimmy, hunched over the bench. "So, Jimmy, what do ya think?"

He slowly looked up. "I don't know." He hesitated, shaking his head. "What I can tell you is that it was a long night, that's for sure." He turned for one last glance at the lighthouse fading in the distance. "If there's something there, anything there, I can tell you this: They walk alone."

Three weeks later, Jimmy and Brian Gurry appeared on our *Ghost Chronicles* radio show on WCCM, where Jimmy's fear factor was tested yet again. As I stared at Maureen over the microphone, I said, "So what are your final thoughts of your night at the lighthouse?"

"I definitely have a different view of what I saw up there," he said with a nervous chuckle. "I don't know if it was a setup or not, but—"

He was not even able to complete his sentence, when the blaring sound of a spectral foghorn disrupted the show. "What the hell was that? Are you guys trying to be funny?"

Lou, the producer, cut in. "That wasn't on our end."

"Maybe you should rethink your words," said Maureen.

Maureen and I could barely contain our laughter. "Jimmy, if I were you, I think I would reconsider my words."

It seems the spirit of the lighthouse took one last shot at Jimmy's dismissiveness.

You can listen to Jimmy's interview on WCCM at *http:// ghostvillage.com/episode-49-halloween-special-new-london -ledge-lighthouse/*.

OUR THOUGHTS

MAUREEN:

The spirits of the lighthouse showed themselves in many ways: technical glitches revealed underlying EVPs and disembodied voices echoed through the headsets of the crew. Karen's EVP—"Help me. I'm cold"—was captured near the stairs, the same spot where a previous investigative team took a picture that produced a mist floating in the night air.

But more importantly, our investigation of New London Ledge Lighthouse may have solved the mystery of Ernie, the lighthouse keeper. My channeling of one of the spirits inhabiting the building revealed that Ernie might well have been a laborer who fell to his death after being locked out on the roof, which is more logical, since there is no record of any lighthouse keeper named Ernie.

RON:

In researching the story for the book, we interviewed Mark Apostolon for his thoughts on the show that eventually was produced for *American Builder* and won an Emmy in 2007.

During the interview, Mark explained some of the strange events that occurred during the editing of the show and the reaction of the viewers to the live broadcast.

While Mark was editing the séance scene, the people nearby who overheard the show were screaming. At that very moment, there was a power outage everywhere else in the building except the editing suite. After this incident, coworkers refused to be near him while he was editing the show.

After the show aired, numerous calls came into the station with complaints that it was demonic and viewers were too scared to watch it. Yet, they wanted to know when it aired next. To me, this proves that what was captured on film was more than just another TV show.

The Sprague Mansion

Part I: The Tour

Case File: 19058893 Sprague Mansion

Location: Cranston, Rhode Island

History: The original house was built by William Sprague in 1790 and remained in the family for four generations. The Sprague family produced two governors and a US senator. They made their fortune through textiles and the A&W Sprague Company. Eventually, the company collapsed, and the house was slated to be torn down by the city. It was saved by the individual efforts of several people and is now home of the Cranston Historical Society.

Reported Paranormal Activity: Strange white mists, apparitions, and creepy feelings of being touched.

Clients: Lydia Rapoza, Dr. Bell, and Cyril Place (members of the Cranston Historical Society).

Investigators: Ron (lead investigator), Maureen (trance medium), Ron Jr. (investigator), Clay (tech manager), and Jim (EVP specialist).

Guests: Marley Harbuck Gibson

Purpose of Investigation: To investigate the mansion as part of a Halloween special radio broadcast event, including the US, UK, and Australia.

I grabbed Maureen's arm and pulled her closer to me as we stood in front of the oversized white sign belonging to the Cranston Historical Society. The cameraman, from behind the camcorder, gave us a thumbs-up, the signal to begin.

"Good evening, everybody, and welcome to the Special Halloween edition of *Ghost Chronicles*. I am Ron Kolek, your host, the gatekeeper to the realm of the unknown, the unexplained, and the unbelievable. New England's own Van Helsing. With me is my cohost, the psychic investigator for the New England Ghost Project, the Queen of Pain, Maureen Wood."

"Hey, how you doing?" she said as she looked at the camera and gave a thumbs-up, mimicking his actions. I couldn't help but wonder if she was a little nervous about being on camera. I smiled as I thought, *She hates being on camera.*

I said, "Today is a really special show: three ghost-hunting groups, on three continents, in three different locations. Haunted Devon from the UK will be investigating the treasury in Plymouth, Devon. Haunted Australia will be investigating the Theatre Royal in Castlemaine, Australia. And the New England Ghost Project will be here, at the Sprague Mansion in Cranston, Rhode Island.

"Maureen, do you know anything about this place?"

"A little bit, but I can't wait to talk to the owners."

"The owners are dead! Then again, I guess that is why *you* are here." I chuckled. "Okay, let's go meet our hosts."

We walked up the stone path to the stately black door of the mansion and rang the bell. The door swung wide, and we were greeted by a familiar face. "Hi, Ron," he said.

"Hello. Maureen, this is Dr. Bell, folklorist and author of *Food for the Dead*." I pointed to the woman standing beside him, "And this is Lydia Rapoza."

In a voice not matching her appearance, she said, "Welcome to the Sprague Mansion, home of the Cranston Historical Society."

Dr. Bell chimed in, "This was the home of the Sprague family. This family is so complex and interesting and a little—"

"Odd?" I said, finishing his sentence.

"Yes, that's a good word to describe them."

"Really? In my experience, most families are a little odd," Maureen added.

Dr. Bell continued, "This family was stranger than most."

One by one we filed into the front room, where we stood in front of a rather large oil painting of a bearded man. "This is Byron Sprague," Lydia said.

"Holy crap! He has more hair on his chin than I have on my whole body. So what is the story on the mansion?" I asked.

"The Sprague Mansion is reportedly Rhode Island's most haunted house. It was built circa 1790 and added to in 1864. It was the home of industrialist William Sprague and his family. If you follow me into the next room, we can see a portrait of Amasa's son, William the fourth," Lydia said as we followed her into the room to the left. "Here is William. He and Amasa were the two richest men in America at the time of the American Civil War."

Barely catching a breath, she continued as she walked through the arch of the adjourning room and stood adjacent to the fireplace. "Although the mansion saw its share of wealth, its opulence was shadowed by death and murder."

My chest tightened, indicating to me that we were not alone. "Honestly, Maureen, I think I can feel something right now."

In agreement, Maureen spoke up, "I can feel it, too."

The door to our left suddenly opened.

Dr. Bell walked over to the door and peered down the empty hall and laughed. "Well, at least the spirits can close the door when they come in."

Slightly shaken, Lydia continued with a little quiver in her voice, "Amasa Sprague was murdered near the mansion on New Year's Eve in 1843. An employee of the mansion, John Gordon, was quickly accused of his murder. In 1845, he was convicted on circumstantial evidence and hung on the gallows. It wasn't until years later that evidence came to light casting doubt on his guilt."

"That's horrible. That poor guy," Maureen interrupted.

"Yes, well, it gets worse. Amasa Sprague's father, William Sprague the second, died in the mansion, choking on a chicken bone at the breakfast table. Kate Chase Sprague, wife of Amasa's son (Governor William Sprague the fourth), went insane. Her son, William Sprague the fifth, committed suicide."

"Holy cow. How can you keep track of the Spragues' drama?" Maureen asked.

"It ain't easy," Dr. Bell said with a smile in his voice.

"Wow, with so many deaths associated with it, do you think the mansion is cursed?" I said.

Dr. Bell paused, choosing his words wisely, said, "It would seem so. . . ."

Lydia broke into the conversation, "If you follow me up the main staircase, I'll give you a tour of the second floor."

We traversed the stairs to the first landing. Maureen paused. "I feel energy starting," she said, waving her hand in front of her, "right about here."

Lydia and Dr. Bell nodded to each other. Lydia then said, "Interestingly, this is where people see a white filmy thing."

———

I stood there for a moment until the energy dissipated. Turning toward Ron, I said, "Whoever was here is gone." I waited for a moment as Lydia, Dr. Bell, and Ron passed by me and continued up the stairs. As we climbed higher, I felt the energy ramping up again.

When we reached the second-floor landing, I followed the group into a small bedroom. Ron immediately went to the closet and pulled out an antique dress on a hanger.

"Those were clothes of little Willy," Lydia said.

"He wore dresses?" I asked.

Lydia grinned. "It was common for boys to wear clothes like this during that time period."

I stifled a laugh. "No wonder they were so messed up."

Still rifling in the closet, Ron pulled out a blue cap with a pom-pom, removed his New England Ghost Project cap, and placed the child's hat on his head.

Lydia, with concern in her voice, said, "That is a very valuable hat."

Ron quipped, "So is my head." With that, he removed the hat and placed it back on the shelf in the closet.

I glanced around the room. This time I took a moment to let the atmosphere of the room sink in. "This is a lovely room, although creepy."

We left William's room and headed to the bedroom across the hall.

"This was Kate's room," Dr. Bell said.

I walked up to a glass shadow box on the far wall. "Is this a hair wreath?" I asked as I stared at the grayish-brown locks braided into a circle.

"Why, yes, it is. That was Kate's. Making wreaths from the hair of a deceased person was popular during that time."

"Oh, yeah. Remember, Maureen, when we went to Georgia. They had a couple of them at the Heritage house."

"Don't remind me. I think they're gross."

Lydia walked into the adjoining dressing room. Placing her hand atop a petite wooden table with a drawer as wide as the length, she said, "This is Kate's dressing table."

"Ooh, maybe we can use this tonight," Ron said.

Taking in his words, I glanced at Ron, whose face lit up like the cat that ate the canary. I couldn't help but wonder what he had up his sleeve. "That's a good idea. In fact, I feel a lot of energy in here—more so in this room than the other."

Lydia, anxious to move on, said, "If you follow me, I'll take you to Amasa's room."

As we entered, I gasped when I saw the antique picture of a man on the bedside table. The likeness to Ron was incredible. I grabbed the frame and shoved it in front of him. "Oh, my God. He looks like you."

Ron looked at it for a moment. "Huh? I was going to say it looks like my father."

Lydia grinned. "That is strange. You know the child's hat with the pom-poms that you put on. That was Amasa's when he was a child."

"Oooh, creepy," I said.

Sensing movement behind me, I turned to find Dr. Bell with an old-fashioned top hat on his head. It was one of several that had been lying on the bed.

"Lydia, do you remember that picture you took of me the last time I put this hat on?"

"Oooh, yes. Do I ever. We got that ghostly image next to you."

"Wow, when you put it on, I can really feel the energy stir," I said.

Ron, not to be outdone by Dr. Bell, grabbed a hat from the bed and placed it on his head. "How 'bout this one?"

"Sorry, Ron. Nothing."

Disappointed, he placed another hat on his head with similar results.

Lydia spun on her heels and grabbed another top hat off the dresser. Before she could even hand it to Ron, he'd already grabbed it out of her hands and placed it on his head.

The second he did, I felt a shift in the energy. "That's the one. You know, I think it's the type of hat that's spurring a reaction."

Now excited, he said, "Cool. Looks like we're going to stir things up tonight. In fact, I know it."

We then followed Lydia up a set of narrow stairs to the cupola, with few results. The next stop, as Lydia described it, was the doll room.

Like a cat slinking up on its prey, Lydia approached the door, stopped, and turned back to us. "This is one of the spookiest rooms in the house."

"Oh, MY God! Maureen, save me," *Ron jokingly cowered.*

"Oh, stop it. Get away from me." *It's never a dull moment with him around.*

Upon opening the door, Ron and I stopped in our tracks. I gazed at the collection of strange-looking dolls peering at me through their lifeless gazes and shivered.

Dr. Bell spoke up, "I have two favorites in here. Two favorites I hate." *Pointing off to the left, he continued.* "The marionette hanging up there and that one," *he said, pointing farther into the room.*

My mind reeled at the sight of a doll with a twisted neck. "Look at that one. It has an adult face painted on it. Now that one's really creepy."

Ron bent at his waist and addressed the dolls as if they were real children. "Hi, guys."

Lydia, who was still leaning on the door handle as if it were holding her up, said, "When we first got the mansion, one volunteer swore up and down that he saw a white filmy thing in this very room. After that, he fled the mansion and told us he would never come back here again."

Dr. Bell spoke up, "And he hasn't. By the way, this used to be the entrance to the servants' quarters. When they built the new addition, they walled it up." *On a roll, he said,* "Has anyone told you about Charlie, the butler?"

"Oooh, Charlie, the butler," *Lydia said.* "We can't forget to tell you about him. Why don't we go to the parlor, and I will tell you all about him."

As she headed down the hall, Dr. Bell chuckled. "She just wants to leave this place. She's always uneasy here."

Still a little freaked out by the dolls myself, I said, "Who can blame her?"

Ron, being Ron, turned back to the room one last time. "Good-bye, kiddies. We will see you later."

We followed Lydia down the corridor and descended the back stairs. I turned the corner and nearly choked, when there in front of me was a dilapidated tombstone leaning against the wall in a doorless closet. "Wow. That's not something you see every day. A tombstone in a house." I read the epitaph out loud, "Amasa Sprague." I continued, "That was his tombstone?"

Dr. Bell replied, "His first one."

Ron laughed, "How many times did he die?"

"Only once. But he was dug up and reinterred and moved closer to the house."

"I'm sure that wouldn't stir things up," I said, finding it difficult to keep the sarcasm out of my voice.

Lydia smiled at me and then walked into the next room. "This is the old parlor. Let me tell you a story. In the 1960s, the city of Cranston wanted to tear this building down. Viola and her husband, Bob Lynch, spearheaded the drive to save the mansion. And as you can see, they were successful. While the mansion was being restored, their son, Bob Lynch Jr., lived in the mansion as a caretaker. One evening in 1968, because they were having paranormal experiences, they decided to get out a homemade Ouija board and see what they could find out. What they got was the story of Charlie. Charlie was a butler here after the Spragues lost their fortune. He had a son who he thought would marry the daughter of the wealthy family he was serving. But it didn't happen. Evidently, he died heartbroken and bitter because they kept getting 'My Land My Land' through the Ouija board.

"In closing, they asked what they could do, and the board spelled out, 'Tell my story.' So since then, we have told his story. But it doesn't end there.

"Viola Lynch passed away before her husband, Bob. Bob became very distraught, and he started painting portraits of her." Lydia pointed to a picture of a woman hanging over the sofa. "This is one of his portraits."

Dr. Bell took over for Lydia. "Several years ago, we had a Halloween party here. Some of the people who came to the party, unbeknownst to us, brought a Ouija board. They started using the board. It spelled out 'I need you, Bob. I want you, Bob.' The interesting thing is that Bob Lynch passed away three months later."

A chill ran up my spine. "Oooh. Interesting. And creepy."

Lydia replied, "And what is really interesting, whoever they were talking to identified themselves through the board as VL. Viola Lynch."

Ron, rubbing his palms together, said, "Wow. Maybe she will be around tonight. We got a whole potpourri of ghosts to choose from. Hopefully, we'll sort it all out before the end of the night."

Just then the radio crackled. Clay's voice came over the speaker. "Hey, Ron, there's someone here to see you."

"Oh, that'll be Cyril," Dr. Bell said as Ron unclipped the radio from his belt. "Who is it, Clay?"

"It's Cyril Place."

"Okay. We're done here. Tell him we'll be right down."

We descended the stairs and went into the kitchen, where we met back up with the team and Cyril, who was patiently waiting for us.

"Hi, Ron. Nice to see you again," Cyril said, extending his hand in a greeting.

Ron shook his hand and introduced Lydia and Dr. Bell to the rest of the team. "This is our crack team of technical guys, Clay, Jim, and Ron Jr."

Clay, preoccupied with adjusting wires, poked his head up from behind the monitor, "Nice to meet you. Sorry, I'm a little distracted right now. We go live in less than forty-five minutes, and I got to get this set up."

"No problem. We're actually headed for the wine cellar right now anyway," Ron replied.

"Ron, I gotta go. So Cyril will show you our infamous wine cellar," Dr. Bell interjected.

"No problem. Thanks for your help."

"Cyril, why don't you lead the way to the wine cellar. Maureen, let's go." I turned to the cameraman. "Why don't you come with us and keep recording?" Ron said.

Standing in the center of the dimly lit wine cellar, I took a deep breath. The musty air filled my lungs. I coughed in a vain attempt to expel the acrid air.

"You okay?" Ron said, lacking sincerity in his voice.

"What do you think?" I said, my voice thick with sarcasm.

Just then, Ron got the cue from the camera guy. "We are now standing in the infamous wine cellar." Ron turned in my direction and continued, "Maureen, this is the first time you've been here, right?"

"Yes."

"Are you feeling anything right now?"

I placed my fingertips to my temple. "My head is pulsating. I could feel the energy walking down here, but the second I walked through those doors, it was unbelievable. It was amplified 100 percent."

Ron turned back to Cyril as the cameraman followed. "So what's the history of this place?"

"Over the past eighty-three years, there have been many reports of people coming into the wine cellar and sensing a presence. Some have even been touched." Cyril walked over to an indentation in the wall. "For the past four years, I have been able to photograph a reoccurring image, but only on infrared film."

Ron interjected. "Really? What does it look like?"

"It looks like a ghostly jellyfish."

"Is it always here, right in front of the wine rack?" I asked.

"Most of the time, but one time I was shooting a publicity shot with Dr. Bell, and it was right up against him, by the door."

Curious, I asked, "Has this image shown up anywhere else in the mansion?"

"No. Just here. I've taken shots of a white mist on the stairs and other spots in the mansion and even hands in the window upstairs. But this image only shows up here."

Cyril pointed to a brick wall behind the wine rack, "Another theory about this room is that there is a tunnel behind this wall. Some believe the tunnel connected the house to the factory, enabling the Spragues the opportunity to spy on their workers."

Not that I like wine, but I couldn't help but ask, "Some people say wine gets better with age, but I'll tell you, the wine in that rack doesn't look too good. Is it drinkable?"

Cyril laughed, "No. All it is good for is to fill up your radiator in your car."

Ron placed his hand to his chin, "I got a great idea!" he said, raising his eyebrow. "Tonight, I am going to send Marley and Jim down here to sit in the dark and try some EVPs."

I chuckled. "Oooh. That is a good idea. But I'm not sure Marley would agree."

Cyril sneered. "Yes, that's not a bad idea at all."

Ending the interview, Ron said, "Thank you, Cyril."

"Thank you, Ron and Maureen. And good luck with your investigation tonight."

Moments later, we returned to the kitchen.

Clay greeted us. "Ron, we're all set. The monitors are up and running. I just have to finish setting up the doll room."

"Sounds good. We'll be here if you need us. Don't forget to bring your radios with you."

"Sure thing. Jim, grab the radio. Ron Jr., grab that extra cable."

Looking through the monitors, we could see Clay running video cables down the hallway. Jim walked behind him taping them to the floor until they reached the camera already set up in front of the doll room. Clay connected the cable and adjusted the camera. He pulled the walkie-talkie off his belt and pressed the button. "Okay, we're live now."

From base camp, I could see Clay through the cameras. He bent over and slowly perused the room filled with dolls. "What's the deal with that one?" he asked. Mumbling to himself, he said, "Wow, this one is really creepy." Clay took a step back and called behind him, "Jim, did you bring your recorders?"

"Oh, crap. I'll go grab 'em. Be right back."

"Are you going to leave me alone in here?" Clay whimpered.

Jim's voice faded away as he walked down the stairs, "Yeah. I said I'll be right back."

Clay's voice erupted in nervous laughter. "I don't think I want to be alone in here."

Judging from Clay's demeanor, I could tell something was up. "Hey, Ron, come here. Look at this."

"What?"

"Take a look at Clay."

As Ron and I peered through the LED monitor, Clay bent over and started chatting with the doll, as if expecting a response. He said, "Hi.

"What's the deal with this one?" Clay said, then extended his hand out to touch the doll, before quickly pulling it back as if it was going to bite him. His attention shifted to another doll. Reaching out again, he gingerly touched its hair that seemed to move slightly.

"Ahhhhhhh!" Clay screamed, jumping back. "Jim! Hurry up!"

"Why? What's wrong?" Jim's voice echoed down the corridor.

"The . . . the . . . the . . . doll. It made a noise when I touched it."

Ron Jr., who had joined us at the base-camp monitor, picked up the radio. "Suck it up, Clay," he said as we all joined in a chorus of laughter.

Ron Jr. continued, "Clay, if you're done playing around, come on down here, back to base camp. We're about to go live."

"I'm on my way."

OUR THOUGHTS

MAUREEN:

During the tour of the Sprague Mansion, I realized that although we all have quirky families, the Sprague family took strange to a whole other level. And it suddenly made me feel very grateful for my own. Another high point of the tour was Clay's horrifying experience in the doll room. Although not necessarily paranormal in nature, it was creepy as hell. Not to mention the years of laughter it has provided us as we tease the poor guy mercilessly.

RON:

During our initial tour of the mansion, Maureen sensed a spot on the stairs where she felt people experienced paranormal activity. She was correct. We were informed that a mist is often sighted there. When we reached Amasa's room, we were greeted by doors that appear to open on their own accord. Finally, on our way to the infamous wine cellar, we found the former homeowner's gravestone in the closet. Right then and there, I knew it was going to be a good night!

The Sprague Mansion

Part II: The Investigation

Case File: 19058894 Sprague Mansion

Location: Cranston, Rhode Island

History: The original house was built by William Sprague in 1790 and remained in the family for four genera- tions. The Sprague family produced two governors and a US senator. They made their fortune through textiles and the A&W Sprague Company. Eventually, the com- pany collapsed, and the house was slated to be torn down by the city. It was saved by the individual efforts of several people and is now home of the Cranston His- torical Society.

Reported Paranormal Activity: Strange white mists, appari- tions, and creepy feelings of being touched.

Clients: Lydia Rapoza, Dr. Bell, and Cyril Place (members of the Cranston Historical Society).

Investigators: Ron (lead investigator), Maureen (trance medium), Ron Jr. (investigator), Clay (tech manager), and Jim (EVP specialist).

Guests: Marley Harbuck Gibson.

Purpose of Investigation: To investigate the mansion as part of a Halloween special radio broadcast event, including the US, UK, and Australia.

As the show opened, we stood in the wine cellar. Looking at Ron with that stupid hat on his head, I could barely contain my laughter. In an attempt to get the ball rolling, I walked over to the indentation in the wall, bobbing my body in between the room and the wine rack.

Ron spoke up, "What on earth are you doing?"

"I'm trying to see if the energy changes from the room to the wine rack."

"Well, does it?"

"No." I almost wish it had.

"You do know there are all kinds of spiders in there."

"Thanks. You are so kind," I said as I began brushing my arms with the palms of my hands. "Eww. Spiders scare me more than anything else." I shivered inwardly as I frantically scratched my head. "Thanks a lot. Now I'm itchy."

"Maureen, what in God's name are you doing?" Marley asked as she and Jim entered the cellar.

"Ah, here comes our next victims," Ron chided.

Marley stopped in her tracks and gave Ron a suspicious look. "I don't like the sound of that."

"Don't you trust me?" Ron said, grinning from ear to ear. "Jim, there's a couple of chairs outside the door. Go grab them and bring 'em in here."

"Sure. But why?"

"So, here's the deal. I want you and Marley to sit in the wine cellar in the dark, with your recorders, to do an EVP session."

"Fine."

"What did you say? Did I hear you correctly?" Marley asked. "I mean, really? With the lights off, too?"

"Yes, you heard me correctly. I didn't stutter, did I?" Ron laughed out loud.

Ron and I shut the lights off, locked the door, and headed back to base camp.

Once back, we began to broadcast while I stared at Marley's and Jim's shadows on the dimly lit monitor. "Eric, are we coming through all right?"

"Everything's fine here at TogiNet."

"Great, thanks." I adjusted the microphone. "For all our listeners out there, I wish you could see Ron. He's grinning from ear to ear. He is finding way too much pleasure in locking Marley and Jim downstairs in that dark, damp, cold basement." I hesitated for only a moment. "God bless you, Marley. That room is very creepy on its own, never mind the energy I felt when we were down there. If we look away and miss anything, maybe if someone in the chatroom sees them bounce around trying to get out, they can give us the heads-up."

"I gave Jim a radio. They should be fine," Ron interjected.

"Look at all those floaties going by. They are probably dust, but it looks spooky," I said pointing to the monitor.

Clay walked up to take a closer look. "We're getting a little lens flare. Can you have them move back farther into the room?"

I took the mic from Maureen. "Jim, can you guys move back a little bit?"

A few seconds later, Jim replied over the radio, "How's this?"

"It's fine."

Something on the screen caught my eye. "Hey, Cyril, take a look at this. Is that your jellyfish next to the left of the wine cabinet?"

"What? What did he say?" Marley's voice rose in panic.

"Never mind, Marley. It's nothing to worry your pretty little head over."

Cyril leaned in for a closer look. "No. Probably just dust."

Addressing our audience, I said, "Looks like Jim is taking readings with his EMF meter. While he's doing that, I'm going to load my infrared film in the camera." I stuck the mic in the stand and reached across the table for the nylon bag. I stuck my hand into the black bag to load the film. "Cyril, you use infrared, don't you?"

"Yes. A lot. It's hard to load. Sometimes I go into the trunk of my car, and it makes it a little easier."

"I tried to get Maureen into the trunk of my car once, but that didn't quite work out either."

"No, it did not, and don't remind me," she said with a laugh.

I changed the subject. "Look at all those orbs scooting around them down there."

Maureen, always reverting to her technical side, said, "I'm sure those are dust particles."

"I don't know. It looks like they have hundreds of spirits zipping around them right now, ready to pluck their eyes out. And suck their brains out their ears."

"You're such an ass." Maureen turned her attention back to the monitors. "Oops, Marley's getting up. Is she supposed to be doing that?"

I picked up the radio and pressed the button. "Wine cellar, this is base camp. Is something going on down there?"

Almost immediately, Jim's voice came back through the radio. "Yes, the temperature's dropping. It's gone down eight degrees in a couple of minutes. It is especially cold to my left."

"That's pretty interesting. All we can see is like a millions orbs all around you."

Jim replied, "Is this completely underground? Are there any windows that could be causing us to freeze?"

"No, it could be caused by all those orbs zipping by you. They're just the lost souls of so many people who have died in the factories that the Spragues tormented over the years, and they are looking to get their revenge on anybody who goes in the wine cellar," I said, my voice trailing off for effect. "Other than that, no reason for the drop in temperature."

"Thanks for that," he grumbled. "How much longer are we going to remain here?"

"Till I tell you, you are done."

A flash of white light illuminated the monitor. "What was that?"

"That was just Marley taking a picture," Jim answered.

"No," I said pointing to the monitor. "What the hell is that?"

I took a closer look. "I am not trying to alarm you, but are you feeling anything near your left shoulder?"

"The shoulder towards Marley? It is very cold."

"There appears to be a mist between you. Marley, by any chance do you feel something touching your hair?"

"Feels like my hair is standing up on the back of my neck," Marley said as her voice began to crack.

"I hate to tell you guys, but I can actually see a face between the two of you."

Marley nervously uttered, "Oh, isn't that great?!"

I raised my voice to emphasize the point, "No, I'm not joking. I'm serious. There is a face, right between you."

Jim spoke up, "Does the face look happy?"

"Ehhh, define happy. Oh, my God. Look at it. You can see the eyes. The nose. It's brutal. I'm serious."

A thought suddenly occurred to me. "Marley, you taking digital photos? Can you review them there?"

After fiddling with the camera, she spoke, "Hey, Ron. There's a rock wall right here, and it looks like a face in it. I'll show it to you when we're done."

"Duh, it might be a face. If it walks like a duck and talks like a duck, it might be a rose." I chuckled. Then, with another look at the monitor, it got serious. "Marley, don't move. It's right there, on your shoulder."

Jim's voice, laced with concern, echoed through the radio, "You are freaking Marley out."

"As well as she should be. How many must die in the name of science. How're you guys holding up? It looks dangerous down there right now."

Marley screeched, "What do you mean dangerous?"

"Look at the freakin' face. And it ain't a happy one."

On the verge of panic, Marley said, "Can we go now? Please?"

"Watch out. The door is locked, and there are spider webs right up above it."

Clay side-stepped Ron and spoke into the mic. "Marley, the door is not locked, and Ron Jr. and I already cleared out the spider webs. So you're fine to leave."

Pushing Clay aside, I said, "Marley, the face has actually changed its position, and it's now looking at you."

"Are you serious?"

"I am serious, dude. I don't make this baloney up," I said.

We watched Marley push the door open. "Okay, I'm out of here."

"Jim, you can come out too before we have to scrape your body off the pavement," I said, over the sound of pounding feet climbing the stairs from the basement. Turning my attention back to the mic, I said, "Okay, Marley. Come over here for an interview." I stuck the mic in front of her pale face, "What did you experience?"

"I am freezing. Feel my hands. I'll tell you, at one point there, I felt like someone was rubbing the back of my neck. My heart's still racing."

"As you can see, Marley, the face is gone. It must have wanted you."

"Stop it, Ron!" She heaved a heavy sigh. "Let me show you what I got with the camera," she said as she clicked through the images, then stopped. "See the face in the stone? Wow, it does look angry."

"It looks eerily similar to the face I saw. Don't lose that. We may need it later."

Turning back to the listeners, I said, "Now it's time to set up for our next experiment. We're going to cut to Haunted Devon in the UK and see how their investigation is doing. And we'll be back. Take it away, Eric."

––––––––––

Ron gave me the signal to begin. "Hello, everyone. We're back. During the break, since Clay was still freaked out from his short experience in the doll room, Ron Jr. graciously volunteered to do a lone vigil."

"Ron, can you hear us now?"

Ron Jr. spoke into the camera's microphone. "Yes, I'm reporting from the doll room. I'm here on a lone vigil. All by myself. In the dark. Surrounded by creepy-looking dolls."

He continued, "I will sit here with the door closed and see what happens. Hopefully, I won't pull a Stewart from Most Haunted *and freak out. I will tell you, I am feeling a little bit weird. I am thinking to myself, what would I do if one of them moved?" Several minutes later he spoke again. "It almost feels as if that giant doll is staring at me." Ron Jr.'s voice cracked as he spoke. The strain was beginning to take its toll. "I know from a psychological point of view, our brains are wired to see humans, and we half expect these dolls to move. If a human doesn't move, it means it's dead." Another few moments of silence, then, "I am not creeped out by this house at all . . . only by a couple of these dolls."*

Ron said, "Clay, grab a radio and join Ron Jr. in the doll room."

In the background, the muffled sounds of Clay's footsteps could be heard. "Sounds like reinforcements are on the way," Ron Jr. said. Even in the darkness we could see Ron Jr. through the infrared camera as he stood up and fumbled for the door knob. He opened the door.

Instantaneously, we could hear Clay screaming.

Clay took a moment to catch his breath. "Damn, you scared me,"
he laughed. "Are you having fun in here?"

"So, Clay, what was that scream? What's happening over there?" I asked.

Clay's voice came over the speaker, "I'm at the doll room now, and other than Ron Jr. stopping my heart when he opened the door as I reached the top of the landing, everything's okay. Can you see me on the camera?"

"Better than you think," I replied.

Still taken aback by the dolls, he yanked the camera out of Ron Jr.'s grasp. Holding the camcorder in his hands, he looked at the screen and scanned the room. "Damn, these dolls are creepy. Wait, what the hell is that?"

"Why? What are you seeing? What's going on?" I said through the radio.

Ron Jr. replied, "It's just Clay. His nerves are little bit on edge right now."

Clay zoomed in with the camcorder on one of the dolls. He called out, "Take a look at this. Even though it's a cloth face, it looks real." He continued, "Look here at this doll. It's three-dimensional."

Ron Jr. replied, "It is just a trick of the camera."

Clay shook his head vigorously. "I don't know. It is a cloth face, but look at the eyes. You can see a reflection in the iris."

I interjected. "I remember. We saw that doll earlier. It is creepy. That's the one with the black dress and the little hat? Hey, by the way, Marley's on the way up. Is she there yet?"

"She just walked in."

Clay cornered Marley. "Look at the image on the camera?"

"Holy crap," Marley said with a slight southern drawl.

Realizing we were broadcasting and wanting to keep our listeners interested, I asked, "Marley, what are you seeing?"

"The doll's face. It looks real." Marley's voice faltered for a moment. "My heart is really beating." She gasped, "I'm short of breath."

Giving her a chance to catch her breath, Clay said, "What is interesting is, even though it's a cloth face, it does look real. Like I said before, three-dimensional."

Clay turned his attention back to Marley, who was still gasping for breath. Concern evident in his voice, he said, "Marley, are you all right?"

As she placed her hand atop her chest, she said, "My heart is racing like a horse. It's just beating so fast." She laughed at her own wit. "I won't ask you to feel it but—"

Clay snickered, "Aww, bummer."

Marley, changing the subject, pointed to one of the dolls. "Look at this one. It's ugly."

Remembering the hideous-looking one in the back of the room, I spoke through the radio. "Is that the one in the back with the adult face and the big red lips?"

"Yeah."

"She's sitting on a chair, and she looks like her neck is broken, right?"

"Yup. That would be the one. Eww. That is disgusting."

Getting a queue from Eric at TogiNet, I said, "Okay, gang. We have to move on. So come on back to base camp now."

Clay, his voice sounding all too eager, said, "I'll be glad to. These dolls give me the creeps."

Marley chimed in, "Me too, and my heart is still racing."

"I can see by the clock, it's time to check in on Australia and see how their investigation is going. So take it away, Eric."

Once again, addressing the audience, I said, "Okay, we're back. Maureen, Cyril, Lydia, and I are in Kate's dressing room. We're going to try a little table tipping with her vanity table. For those who are not familiar with table tipping, it's a means to communicate with spirits. Everyone places their fingers gently on the table while asking questions, and the table will respond with movement. At least we hope."

Maureen spoke up as we all placed our fingers atop the table. "I'm feeling the energy right now. Let's see if we can make a connection."

As we stood around the table, she asked, "Are there any spirits with us in this room right now? We would like for you to make your presence known." Shaking her head, she turned to me, "I can feel the energy. It's starting."

I added, "Is there anyone here? Please give us a sign."

Maureen spoke up again, "I'm beginning to feel a rocking on the top of the table. Anybody else?"

Cyril's voice erupted in excitement, "YES!"

Maureen's head fell forward as she began to channel.

"Who is here with us?" I asked.

Maureen murmured as the table began to rock to and fro, its legs lifting off the hardwood floor. "I feel that Kate is with us now." As if in pain, she began to groan. "He won't leave me alone." Maureen's voice grew louder, more adamant. "Go away. Leave me alone."

Lydia spoke up, "Kate, is your husband William with us right now?"

"Yes. Mmmm. This is mine. This is mine I say!" Maureen bellowed.

"She's trying to speak through me. But this other energy, it's just so heavy," she said, gasping for breath. "It's like someone else is pulling her back. Wait." She moaned in pain. "It's not her husband right now. It's her father."

The table rocked violently as the drawer flung open. "My right arm is going numb."

"Break it. Break it, Maureen." As if she heard my words, through grunts and groans, she pushed herself off the table and fell back against the wall with a thump.

I reached out and placed my hand on her shoulder. "Are you all right?"

Through the seething pain, she replied, "Damn it! My arm's completely numb."

"That will wake you up," I said, trying to break the tension of the room.

"The spirit blocking her was extremely angry with Kate. He doesn't want her talking. There's some reason why she left. And he doesn't want the secret out."

Realizing we needed to take a break, I said, "I think we're done here. Let's turn it back over to Eric while we catch our breath."

———

After Maureen regained her strength, we moved to another room to continue with our next segment. "We're back. I'm here with Clay and Maureen, and we're standing in Amasa's bedroom. Maureen has her pendulum out, and she's going to attempt to make contact." I glanced at her. "Maureen, are you feeling anything right now?"

"Yes," she said as she waved her hand in the air waist high. "He's standing right by my side."

"Really?"

"Yeah. Feel right here."

Placing my hand next to Maureen, I was momentarily stunned. It was as if I had stuck it in a refrigerator. "Wow, it seems really cold there." I turned to Clay. "Get the temperature sensor and take some readings."

As Clay began to take readings, I asked, "Maureen, can you sense who it is?"

She stared off into space. Then placing her free hand to her temple, she said, "It's Amasa."

Intrigued with the opportunity, I said, "Amasa, do you know who murdered you?"

Maureen chuckled. "Funny, I was going to ask the same question. And yes, he does."

"Was it Gordon?"

As if mentally repeating my question, she paused, then replied, "No. It was someone who worked at the mill."

"Is that why you recognize him?"

"Yes," she said as the pendulum continued to swing wildly.

I continued, "Do you believe your brother had anything to do with your death?"

"Yes," she said, with the pendulum confirming her response. "Clay, put your hand right here under the pendulum. Do you feel it?"

Clay reached out gingerly. "Oh, my God. Yes, it's freezing."

I glanced down at the recorder on the table. "Clay, how come that recorder is not recording. Isn't it on Vox?"

"Yeah, it is."

"Then why isn't the light lit?"

Clay picked up the recorder and began inspecting it. "I don't know, unless the batteries are dead; but they can't be, because we put all new batteries in the equipment tonight."

"Whatever the reason, it's not recording."

Maureen interjected, "Ron, he's gone."

"Bummer, I guess he didn't like the distractions," I said as I glanced at the clock on the wall. It was almost midnight, and we were running out of time. "Okay, like Cinderella at the ball, when the clock strikes midnight, we're out of here. It's time to wrap it up.

"Well, it's been a great night. And I can't believe the time went by that fast. I want to thank you all for listening and for joining us on this unique journey into the realm of the unknown, the unexplained, and the unbelievable. We especially want to thank TogiNet and the BBC for allowing us to broadcast on this Halloween night; Haunted Devon and Haunted Australia for accompanying us on this journey; Lydia, Dr. Bell, and Cyril for hosting us here at the Sprague Mansion. But most of all, we want to thank our team for making this all possible. Good night, God bless, and Happy Halloween."

OUR THOUGHTS

MAUREEN:

Cohosting a radio show over three continents was an amazing experience, especially when you consider how young the US is, as compared to the UK, for instance. Yet, on all three continents, each team was successful at encountering various levels of paranormal activity. Our investigation at the Sprague Mansion proved especially active—especially for poor Marley and Jim, who braved it out in the wine cellar and ended up with an eerie mist/ face appearing between the two of them.

RON:

During our initial walkthrough, I realized what a great night it was going to be. It started off with the door opening by itself in Amasa's room and ended with Clay's fearful encounter in the doll room.

Turtle Mound

Case File: 1905325 Turtle Mound

Location: Andover, Massachusetts

History: Turtle Mound is eighty-six feet wide, ninety-six feet long, and fifteen feet tall. It was given its name because it resembles a reptile. The mound looks like a hill of stone but has chambers and a passageway of unknown origins.

Reported Paranormal Activity: Strange feelings; sudden, unexplained changes in temperature; the feeling of being watched.

Client: Denise McCarthy (owner).

Investigators: Ron (lead investigator), Maureen (trance medium), Ron Jr. (investigator), Thermal Dan (thermal imaging specialist), Clay (tech manager), Tom S. (videographer).

Press: Rosemary Ford (reporter for *Andover* magazine) and her photographer.

Purpose of Investigation: To investigate the mysterious Turtle Mound.

S*itting in the small, upscale country kitchen, the brass lamp illuminated the face of Denise McCarthy and cast a shadow upon those who stood behind her. This interview/investigation was a first for* me, seeing that it was only minutes away from where I lived. Even though I had grown up in Andover, I had never heard of Turtle Mound. Just goes to show, sometimes you don't have to go too far to find a mystery.

Ron placed the small recorder atop the kitchen table and began, "We are here with Denise McCarthy of Andover, Massachusetts." He took a breath and then said, "So Denise, what is your relationship with Turtle Mound?"

"My dad bought this property in 1960, and he built this home in 1966. He passed away about a year ago. He knew a lot about the mound and gave tours of the rock. I have a picture of him over there, on the hutch."

I interjected. "Denise, what was your father's name?"

"Dennis F. McCarthy."

I continued to ask questions, "Why is the rock called Turtle Mound?"

"It got the name because it is in the shape of a turtle."

"Denise, as you know, I live in Andover as well. I'm really fascinated with Turtle Mound. Can you tell us a little bit more about the property?"

"Turtle Mound, from the information we have received, was created by either the Algonquin or the Irish monks."

"Wow, that's quite a diverse assumption. How did you come up with that?"

"There are a lot of theories from different people who have studied the mound. Arrowheads have been found here. Some believe the Indians held people captive here. And there is one man who has studied the mound and believes it has its origin from Suffolk, England. There are similar mounds there, where they used to keep their cattle in it. All are located by water. Just like this one."

"Who were the most recent people to have studied the mound?"

"New England Antiquities Research Association. They came up here in 2002. They have gathered quite a bit of information from *their investigation. They believe that Turtle Mound is tied in with a lot of places around New England. They also discovered that there is someone buried on the lake side of the mound. It was uncovered by an archaeologist. They believe whoever is buried there is interred with some kind of a saber."*

"Really?"

"Yes, through their research, they discovered that both the Algonquin and the Irish monks were buried with some type of weapon to carry with them into the next life."

"Hmmm, that is interesting."

"The problem is that there are so many different theories about the mound that today it still remains a mystery."

Ron, growing impatient, spoke up, "Okay, unless you have anything else you want to tell us, let's take a crack at this place and see if we can solve the mystery of Turtle Mound."

I zipped up my rain jacket and slipped the hood over my head as we followed Denise out the back door. It took us only a minute or two to reach a small stone wall that bordered the back of her yard. We quickly stepped over the rain-slicked wall and onto a narrow path that led us into the thick woods. It wasn't long before we reached the first chamber of the mound.

We entered the chamber and formed a small semi-circle facing the back of the cave. Ron asked, "Maureen, do you have your pendulum?"

"Yeah," I replied, holding it up. "This time I don't need to borrow yours." I snickered.

"Are you feeling anything here?"

Ron's voice trailed off in my mind as the light energy I'd felt upon walking in suddenly increased. "I am now, Ron." No sooner had I responded than a swift, sharp pain enveloped my head, indicating to me an increasing presence. This was not what I had expected.

"I am not getting anything on my EMF meter." Ron's agitation was evident in his voice.

This is not the first time that the meter failed to read the energy I was picking up on. I knew what I was feeling. To ease his mind, I began to dowse. "Is there someone with us here tonight?" I asked.

Yes.

"Is there more than one spirit with us tonight?"

Not waiting for a response, Ron spoke up, "For those who aren't familiar with dowsing, that would be yes."

I looked at Maureen and noticed a distant look in her eyes. "Maureen?" *I didn't like where this was going.*

Still no reply, I continued, "Maureen, are you with us?"

Eyes now closed, she groaned in response.

"Okay, what's going on?"

Maureen slowly opened her eyes and stared at me. "Sorry, Ron. I am just trying to get a feel on what they are trying to do."

"Do they want to communicate, or are they just curious?"

"I'm not sure, but I do think there were Indians and not monks here. They were buried here."

"Ron, there's something wrong with the camera," Clay said as he fiddled with the infrared.

"Is the autofocus going in and out?"

"Yes."

"That's a good indication that there's something here." I turned my attention back to Maureen. "Are there any active spirits here?"

She slowly nodded her head in response.

"Can the spirits leave, or are they grounded?"

"Yes, they're grounded. They stay here. As a matter of fact, I feel like they are connected to Salem."

"Salem, New Hampshire?"

"Yes, I feel that same energy." Maureen looked at me as if she were reluctant to continue. "Do you remember the spirit that followed us around there?"

"Oh, yeah. Do I ever?!" I thought to myself, *Do I remember? How could I ever forget?*

"Is he aware of who we are?"

"No, not as far as I can tell."

A feeling of relief crossed my mind, "Oh, that's good."

Maureen's eyes darted from wall to wall. "The energy is all around us. Some of it is the spirit. The rest of it is imprinted energy."

"Imprinted? Like the stone is holding a memory?"

"Exactly."

"I'll tell you what. Feel the wall and tell me what you get."

Maureen raised her hand and placed it on the cold, damp stone. She closed her eyes once again. After what seemed like hours but couldn't have been more than a few moments, she spoke. "I feel ceremonial energy. I can hear chanting."

Another few seconds passed before she spoke again. "I sense it was a gathering place. Where they came from different locations to meet and perform various ceremonies."

"Is it male energy or mixed?"

She opened her eyes. "Mixed, but mostly male. I also get the feeling that they were defenders or protectors of this place."

"Are you sensing anything else?"

"No, not at the moment."

"All right. I think we're done here. Let's go outside and walk around the stone." I turned to Denise who was standing next to the entrance of the cave. "So, Denise, have you ever been out here at night in the rain?"

"No, I have not. This is a first."

"Okay, then. Let's do it." With the rest of the group in tow, we walked out into the rain along the perimeter of the mound until we approached the large tunnel. I turned back to Denise again. "How far does this tunnel go?"

She sniffled. "It goes all the way through the rock."

I raised my voice to be heard above the rain. "Come on, guys. Catch up. We're going in." Stepping deeper into the tunnel, I slipped on the wet leaves, barely preventing myself from falling. I yelled to the team, "Watch your step. The rocks are wet and slippery."

I glanced at Maureen, who was now by my side, and I could tell that she was already connected with whatever or whoever was there. By the time the rest of the group had entered the tunnel, Maureen was ready to speak. "Ron, I'm picking up on some more energy."

A little apprehensive to let Maureen channel with what we had encountered in Salem, I decided to change gears. "Okay, let's try something different," I said as I took my digital recorder from my jeans pocket. Addressing Denise and Rosemary, the magazine reporter, I said, "I'm going to try to communicate with the spirits through the recorder. This is called EVP—electronic voice phenomenon.

Everybody, please be quiet," I said as I pushed the record button.

"Are there any spirits here now?"

After waiting a few seconds, I continued, "Are you Native American?"

Once again, I waited, giving the spirit a chance to respond on the recorder. "Are you associated with the Spirits at Mystery Hill in Salem?"

A few moments later, I played back the recorder as everyone gathered around. Much to my dismay, there were no replies. *I suck at EVPs.*

Reluctantly, I asked Maureen, "What about you? You picking up on anything?"

A grin of satisfaction crossed her lips. "I'm sensing them gathering here, eating. And I think there's a specific reason why that person Denise told us about is buried here. I believe he was the protector, the one who was in charge."

"Do you feel that they can leave this place?"

Before Maureen could respond, Clay's voice interrupted us. "I heard something out there. Look. What are those two red lights in the woods?"

Looking out the entrance at what appeared to be two red eyes, I said, "Holy crap, what the hell is that?"

"Damn. They're gone," Clay exclaimed.

"Wow, that was strange!" *It was strange. More than anyone here could even know. In fact, the first investigation I'd done on Mystery Hill in Salem, New Hampshire, we had the same experience. Two red eyes in the woods that had quickly disappeared. Maybe these places are more tied together than we think.*

"You know, Ron. It feels like there is something more than ground under this place," Clay said as he stomped his foot on the stone floor of the tunnel.

I replied, "Yes, I agree. I felt the same thing when we were in the other chamber. The ground felt hollow."

"Look here at the walls. It seems like these stones were placed here afterwards. To me, it looks like they were hiding something, or something has been walled up." Clay maneuvered the infrared (IR) camera, wedging it between the crack in the stones. "I'm trying to use the camera to see if I can peer into it."

"Can you see anything?" I asked.

"No, it's not working."

"Bummer."

Maureen, still connecting to the energy, spoke up again, "I almost feel like there is another body here or somewhere else around here."

"Could this be an elaborate burial mound?" Clay asked.

I took my flashlight and jammed it into a small crevice in the wall. "Hey, Clay, check this out!"

I stepped back to make room for Clay. Stepping up to the wall, he peered into the opening. "See, that's what I was saying. There seems to be open space behind the wall."

"See if you can put your hand in there and feel how far back it goes."

"No way! I see a web in there, and I do not like spiders."

Maureen grimaced and said, "I hate spiders."

"For crying out loud, you don't like spiders, you don't like dolls. Geez, Clay. I'll do it. Van Helsing fears nothing."

"Go ahead. Better you than me."

I stuck my hand into the opening. "I feel spiders."

"Eww," Maureen screeched.

"I can't reach the back wall, so I don't know how far back it goes." I turned to Maureen. "What are you getting now?"

"Besides being creeped out by spiders? I feel energy. But I felt it more in the other chamber and underneath us than right here."

"Did you bring your crystal skull with you?"

"No, I left it at the house."

"Oh, for God's sake, Maureen."

"It's not like it is a mile away."

"Where's Ron Jr.?" He stepped forward. "Ron, we need a runner. Can you go back to the house and get the crystal skull?"

"Ron, can you get my recorders too," Clay added. "They're in the trunk of my car, in the green bag."

"Sure," he replied. "But before I go, take a look at this wall. Can you see how it seems to be built around something?"

I took a step closer. "Yeah, you're right. This place is strange. It almost looks as if something was walled up in there as well."

Ron Jr. stepped out into the rain. I turned to Denise and asked, "Do you know anything about this?"

"No. Sorry. But there are some stairs that lead to the top of the mound. Do you want to check them out? They're outside to the left. Just follow the path."

The beam of my flashlight darted on the ground in front of us until we reached a large opening. "Oh, cool. It's another chamber."

Climbing inside, I couldn't help but notice the differences between this chamber and the first one we had encountered. I stood and appraised the situation. "I'm sorry, but there is no way that this was built by Indians. Look at the marks on the stone." As I attempted to illuminate them, my flashlight went out. "Damn, it just went dead.

As the rest of the group entered the chamber, I said, "Watch your step. My flashlight just died."

Clay, peering through the IR camera, said, "Hey, check this out. This is cement."

Maureen responded, "I don't get much energy in here. In fact, barely anything. I think this was added on later."

"This is definitely much later," Clay replied.

"Yeah, I think they stored things here. Maureen, do you remember that crypt in the woods that everybody thought was a tomb. The one where we figured out that it was actually a root cellar? Well, I think this is similar."

"Yeah, I remember that one."

I took a moment to examine the walls of the chamber and found a rather large hole. "What the hell? Look at this. You can see behind this stone, and it goes on and on. Way back."

"Want me to shoot the camera in there, Ron?" Clay asked.

"You can do that? There are spiders in there, though." I chuckled.

"Ha-ha. That's okay as long as I don't have to stick my hand in there." Clay tried repeatedly to place the lens of the camera into the opening. "Aw shucks, the camera won't fit in there, but it definitely goes way back."

"That's okay," I said, peering over his shoulder. "Where's Thermal Dan?"

"Right here, Ron," he said, stepping out of the darkness.

"Have you been able to pick anything up on the thermal imaging tonight?"

"No, not so far."

Unable to hide my disappointment, I decided to change tactics. "All right, let's go on top. Denise, which way to the stairs?"

She replied, "Out here. Like I said before—just follow the path."

Clay took a step back and let out a laugh. "Go ahead, Ron. Brave the way."

With Maureen and me in the lead, we stumbled our way through the darkness. As we reached a rock formation that jutted farther out from the mound, she asked, "Is this it, Ron?"

"No."

"It looks steppish to me."

"Well, it might look steppish, but they ain't stairs," I said as I pointed just ahead. "There they are."

We cautiously climbed the stone steps to the top of the mound. As Maureen reached the top, she froze for a moment. "Oh, this is cool." The excitement in her voice was evident. "This is really, really cool."

As I watched Maureen meandering around the top, apprehension grew. "Okay. Hold up, Maureen. At least wait until we get everybody up here that's coming."

"Stop being a worrywart. I actually got more energy below than up here up top."

"That would make sense. The stone in the chambers should hold more energy than here in the open where it would dissipate." I continued, "Are we all here?"

A chorus of yups answered my question.

"You know what's funny, Ron. I feel the energy low here, like it is below us. Wait. Someone's coming."

"Where?"

"I said someone's coming. A spirit. Right behind Clay. Never mind. It backed off."

My chest tightened as I pictured in my mind all of the things that could possibly go wrong. "Maureen, be careful not to get too close to the edge. It's a long way down, and there are lots of jagged rocks down there.

"You know, Ron. This is a cool place, but I'm getting nothing," she said. Then out of the blue, she suddenly crouched down.

"Okay. Wait. Why are you crouching?"

"Because I can feel energy below me, and I am trying to see if I angle down lower if it will get stronger. And it is."

"So do you think it's residual energy?"

"Yes, like memories and impressions of everything that has taken place. This mound was much smaller at the time," she said as she swiped at the air in front of her.

"What are you waving at?"

"Bugs."

"There are no bugs. What kind of stupid bugs would go in the rain?" Suddenly, my uneasiness grew. "You're getting very close to that ledge, you know."

"I know. I was . . . ah . . . someone . . . ahh." She paused. "I can't even talk. The energy is just so strong."

"Is someone here?"

Without answering my question, she removed the pendulum from her jacket pocket and held it in her hand.

She asked, "Is there someone here with us right now?"

Mimicking the actions of the crystal, she replied, "Yes."

"Are you a Native American spirit?"

"Yes."

"Are you a male?

"Yes," she said, her voice beginning to slur.

I took another look at Maureen and could see her demeanor changing. Experience told me that she was on the edge of channeling.

I raised my voice and spoke sternly. "Maureen, you do not want to make contact right now. You are crouched on the edge of a cliff. Tell him we will talk downstairs. Maureen, are you listening to me? Maureen?" *Oh shit, this is not good.*

"Push him out."

Maureen began rocking back and forth on her heels, oblivious to my commands.

"Maureen, push him out. This is not a good place. Maureen." Still no reply.

"Ron, she's on the edge of a cliff," Dan said.

Damn it. It's too freakin' late.

"I'm speaking to the spirit. This is not your body. Please leave." I continued, "I mean you no harm. But this is not your body. Please. Leave."

Maureen's voice deepened as she began to chant, "Ne' sa tin. Na 'wa kwa."

With my concern deepening, I reached out. She edged backward, closer to the edge. Her voice grew louder, "Chi ga kwa. Chi ga kwa."

With her dangerously close to the edge, my fear for her safety grew. "Leave this body. Now!"

"Ne' sa tin. Na 'wa kwa. Chi ga kwa," Maureen continued.

I looked at Dan and could tell by his eyes that we were on the same page, and we had to act fast. I raised my hand, showing three fingers.

He nodded in silent agreement.

One . . . two . . . three.

In unison we reached out and grabbed Maureen, pulling her forward, away from the edge, slamming her to the ground.

She struggled violently as we held her down. "Leave this body." With her still struggling beneath our grasp, I continued, "Leave this body. I command you. I command you to leave this body. It's not your own."

As her resistance waned, I called to her, "Maureen!"

"Maureen!"

She coughed and cleared her throat. "I'm here. What the hell? I was trying to push him out," she said as we released the grip on her. "You didn't even give me a chance to push him out," she snapped.

"Sorry, we couldn't wait. You were dangerously close to the edge."

Dan chimed in. "Ron's right, Maureen. Take a look down there. You really didn't want to go over the edge."

"You all right, Maureen?" Rosemary asked out of the darkness.

"Yeah, thanks." With a tone of annoyance in her voice, she continued, "Ron, you didn't even give me a chance."

"Well, sorry, but I wasn't going to take the risk. You getting impaled on the rocks might be a little hard to explain to Steve."

Maureen once again had a far-off look in her eyes, making me aware that she was still not fully in control. "Maureen?"

"I'm here. But he's back again, trying to come through."

"Too bad. Let's get out of here."

A guttural cough erupted from Maureen.

"Are you okay?"

"Yes, well, I don't know," she said, between coughs.

"Well, by the sound of it, it doesn't appear so. Take your time, but keep him away."

Her coughing turned to hacking. "My lungs hurt," she said as she inhaled deeply into the night air, appearing to regain her strength. "I'm okay."

Dan and I grabbed her arms and lifted Maureen to her feet. "Sorry about throwing you down, but we really didn't have much of a choice," I said. "It was a tricky balance. If I provoked him, you might have gone backwards."

"Okay, let's get out of here."

A few minutes later we assembled in the first chamber together.

"Ron Jr., can we have the skull, please?"

"Here you go, Dad."

"Okay. Here's the plan. We're going to try and use the crystal skull to draw the energy in."

Rosemary spoke up from the mouth of the chamber. "Why would you do that, with everything you just went through?"

"That's why we're here, right? Because that's what we do."

"Maureen, you and I will hold the skull," I said as I placed the crystal between our hands. "Dan, you stand over here," I said with a nod. "And observe with the thermal imager."

I continued, "All right, we need quiet now. Denise, since you are affiliated with the site, I want you to ask the questions."

We all took our places, and Denise began to ask questions.

Maureen, hands on the skull and head down, responded to each of them.

We soon determined that the mound had at one time been in the possession of Native Americans. The spirit continued to tell us that there was someone buried there and that they were aware of who Denise's father was.

Dan, still peering through the screen of the thermal imager, spoke up, "Ron, are you getting something from the skull?"

Maureen erupted in a cough.

I jumped in, "Maureen, is this the same spirit from before?"

"Yes," she replied, between coughs.

"Does Dennis's spirit come here?"

"Yes. He has come here before, but not for a while," Maureen said.

"Do you like Dennis?"

"Yes, because he took care of this place. He loved it, and he had so much interest in it."

Between the sound of Maureen's coughing and the pelting of the rain, it was becoming difficult to concentrate. "I think we're going to end it. Is there anything else you would like to say?" I waited for a moment. "No? Okay. We're done."

Almost immediately, Maureen began to chant again. "Mi'tig wa ki. Mi'tig wa ki."

"Oh, no. We don't have time for this. Thank you for speaking with us. But we really have to leave."

As if the spirit heeded my request, Maureen's chanting tapered off.

Everyone began to chat among themselves. As I headed toward the opening of the chamber, Dan tapped me on the shoulder. "Ron, can I show you something?"

"Sure. Did you get something on the thermal imager?"

"Take a look at this. See, this is you and Maureen holding the crystal skull. See. It's warm because you are holding it. But look closely. Remember when I said, 'Are you getting something from it?' Well, look at your hands. They are getting hotter and hotter. They actually begin to shake. And see here. It looks like it is going up your arms."

"Oh, wow, that is cool."

"Watch this. When you say we are going to break it, watch what happens. The skull goes black except for the eyes. It almost seems that whatever energy was going into the skull jumped into Maureen. See? Look at your eyes, Maureen. And that's when you started chanting again."

We all jumped at the sound of thunder clapping in the distance.

"Okay, everybody. I think it's a wrap.

"Denise?" I said calling out into the darkness.

She stepped back inside the opening. "Here I am."

"Why don't you lead the way back?"

"Okay, but please be careful. The rocks are very slick from all this rain we had."

The events of the night raced through my mind as we journeyed back to the house. Although we had uncovered many clues, it seems the mystery of Turtle Mound remains the same. A mystery.

AMERICA'S STONEHENGE

An archeological site in Salem, New Hampshire. It is a maze of chambers, walls, and ceremonial stone structures. It includes an astronomical calendar and a structure of what appears to have been a sacrificial altar. It is reportedly the oldest man-made construction in the United States, dating back four thousand years.

OUR THOUGHTS

MAUREEN:

Even though I grew up in Andover, Massachusetts, it wasn't until I received a phone call from a friend who told me all about Denise and the stone structure that existed on her property that I learned about Turtle Mound. Just goes to show you that you don't have to travel far to find a mystery. The investigation at Turtle Mound was unusual, even for me. I'm not sure what I expected to experience that night. However, chanting in Native American and being tossed to the ground like a sack of potatoes by Ron and Dan were certainly not what I'd had in mind. Then again, I can see their point. If I've never thanked you properly, Ron and Dan (I know you are listening from beyond), both my husband and I thank you kindly for keeping me from doing a swan dive off a rocky ledge.

RON:

I was thankful for being given this opportunity to do a rare investigation on an ancient structure. And although it rained all night, it was still an interesting experience. Even though we found little physical evidence, there were enough similarities to America's Stonehenge that I could not help but believe that we were dealing with the same spirits.

Attack of the Puckwudgie

Case File: 1904083 Freetown State Forest

Location: Assonet, Massachusetts

History: Freetown State Forest is located in the southern portion of the Bridgewater Triangle. This isolated spot was used as a dumping grounds for murder victims. Rumors persist of Satanic rituals and human sacrifice carried out in these dark woods, the reported home of the mythical Puckwudgie.

Reported Paranormal Activity: Ghost lights, eerie mists, slithering shadows, and disembodied screams. Visitors suffer from suicidal tendencies, depression, and an uneasy feeling of being watched.

Clients/Press: Andrew Lake (*Greenville Paranormal*), Chris Balzano (author).

Investigators: Ron (lead investigator), Maureen (trance medium), Ron Jr. (investigator), Thermal Dan (thermal imaging specialist), Clay (tech manager), Jim (EVP specialist), Stacy (investigator).

Purpose of Investigation: To provide author Chris Balzano the experience of working with a paranormal team in the outdoors for his book, *Picture Yourself Ghost Hunting*.

Length of Investigation: Evening hike lasting a maximum of five hours.

PUCKWUDGIE

The legendary Puckwudgie is found in New England and other parts of the country. It's described as a three-foot-tall being with slightly elongated arms and covered with hair. This elusive shape-shifter has a wolf-like snout and a paunch belly. It has long been feared because of its reputation for luring unsuspecting victims deep into the forest to steal their souls.

I stood ankle deep in the wild grass as the chilling April wind gently bent the blades against my jeans. My intuition told me that the serene scene was nothing more than a façade. I knew the apprehension that had overtaken me on the drive here was a forewarning of the night that lay ahead. Even Ron's attempt at driving, the constant jerking and swerving from one lane to another, was not enough to distract me from my dire thoughts. What were we in for?

The sound of laughter closed in around me, snapping me back to reality.

"Let's get this party started," Ron said, stepping closer to me and the rest of the team. "Maureen, got your pendulum?"

Crap. I knew I forgot something. "Ah."

In one quick gesture, Ron yanked his rhodonite pendulum out of his pocket. "I swear, sometimes I'm nothing more than your purse."

I snatched the chain from his hand and began to dowse.

He gazed at me and impatiently spat, "Is there anything here?"

"Anything?" I responded. "Do you think we can be a little clearer? Remember, garbage in, garbage out."

"Fine. Are there any Puckwudgies here?"

With his words, the air shifted. The pink stone that had felt light moments before hung heavy in my hand, weighted. The pendulum swung to and fro.

Within seconds, the stone spun counterclockwise, indicating yes.

"Okay. Well, where are they?" Ron asked.

The pendulum began to swing toward the setting sun. "This way," I said, pointing to a narrow path, overgrown with prickly bushes and rotted logs.

I felt "it" again. I didn't need the pendulum to tell me that we were heading directly for whatever lay ahead. I must be out of my mind.

Not trusting me to keep his prized possession safe, Ron reached out and grabbed his pendulum, stuffing the stone back into the front pocket of his jeans. "Let's go."

With Ron and me in the lead, we stumbled through dead trees and tangled vines, disappearing into the forest. With each step deeper into the woods, the camaraderie and jovial attitude of the team began to dissipate.

In the silence, I found myself secretly hoping that the methodic crunching of the breaking branches beneath our feet disguised my labored breathing. I was out of shape, and it was becoming more evident by the minute.

Clay shouted from the rear of the group. "Do you know where you're going?"

Not really. But how could I say that I, too, was beginning to wonder. I stopped and turned toward Ron, his face lit by the dial of his digital watch.

"Got your pendulum?"

He grunted, pulled it from his pocket, and dropped it in the palm of my hand.

I grasped the chain and began to dowse. The pendulum swung, pointing to the barely distinguishable path before us. If the reading was accurate, we were headed in the right direction, but deep down I had my doubts.

Chris and Andrew stepped forward. "Ron, our cameras won't work in the dark," Chris said. He paused for moment. "We have to go back to the car. Do you want to meet us at the ledge?"

"Okay," Ron said removing the walkie-talkie from his belt and handing it to Chris. "Here, take this in case you get lost."

"Yeah, right." Chris snickered as he and Andrew did an about-face and vanished into the darkness.

Grabbing the pendulum out of my hand, Ron stuffed it back into his pocket. After hesitating for a moment, he said, *"Let's go."*

Our flashlights lit up the path before us as we continued our journey. As we trudged ahead, Dan, with the thermal imager, and Clay, with the infrared camera, scanned the horizon. *"Are you guys picking up anything? I feel like we're being watched."* My skin crawled. I didn't know what it was, but it wasn't anything I'd ever felt before.

Dan replied, *"I see something, but it's fleeting."*

The path before us grew thicker, and even the darkness grew darker.

I suddenly felt disoriented. *"Ron, give me your pendulum."*

"Okay," he said, as he reached into his pocket. *"Crap."*

"What's the matter?"

"My pendulum's gone," he grumbled. *"Maureen, are you sure you don't have it?"*

Stacy chimed in, *"She doesn't have it. I saw you put it in your pocket."*

"Well, I don't have it now."

"Oh, my God. Don't you think it's weird? I mean, aren't Puckwudgies supposed to lure you into the forest? Maybe this is their plan," Stacy continued.

"Whatever."

Ron called out to his son. *"Hey, Jr., why don't you take the radio and scout ahead."*

Ron Jr. took the radio and bolted, the beam of his flashlight fading into the night. Soon after, his voice chirped through the radio. *"There's a road up here."*

We followed his path. Within minutes, we stepped out of the woods onto a gravel road. A sigh of relief escaped my lips.

Finally. Signs of civilization.

We stood for a moment while we waited for everyone to exit the woods.

Ron spoke up, "Which way, right or left?"

Without a pendulum, I improvised. I reached back and unclasped the silver chain and pendant from around my neck and began to dowse with it.

"This way, I think," I said, pointing to the right.

My feet grew heavy as we walked for what felt like miles. The silence of the forest grew louder as the conversations grew silent. It was as if each member of the team sensed the shift in the atmosphere around us. Ron's flashlight went dead, and everyone stopped in their tracks. Just then Ron Jr.'s voice echoed in the night. "Dad, come here."

With that, Ron ran ahead.

Whatever creature had been following us for the past few hours came closer.

It felt stronger.

Violent.

"There's something out there," I said. "There's something out there watching us."

Thermal Dan stopped in his tracks, swiveled to his right, and peered into the dimly lit screen of the thermal imager. "Hey, Clay. Check this out. What the hell is that?"

My forehead pulsed. My heart raced as the voices of the team grew dim. Something was upon us. And whatever it was, it wasn't pretty.

Clay stepped closer to Dan, gazing at the black-and-white image before him. "What the hell is that? Is that what you're talking about?" Clay pointed to the screen. "There between the trees."

"I don't know what it is, but this dark shadow has been following us for a while. Almost as quick as it appears, it disappears—as if it knows I can see it."

"Oh, man, check that out. What is that?" Clay's voice sped up. His finger tracing on the screen. "Two eyes. A mouth. Hair? See that developing. What is that? Holy crap. It's coming this way."

Everything happened at once. Whatever it was hit me like a Mack truck.

Clay reached out, "Maureen? Maureen, are you okay?"

I staggered.

My consciousness faded.

"Ron. Ron, you better get back here!" Clay screeched.

I rushed back to the group. "What? You see something?"

"No. It's Maureen."

Turning around, I quickly focused my attention on Maureen. She was hunched over, hands on her thighs, perched on an embankment. While the group closed in around her, calling her name, jeering to her like a crowd in a schoolyard fight.

I removed my duffel bag and tossed it to Stacy.

"Give her space," I said as I gestured to the team.

She emitted a snakelike sound. Through clenched teeth, she continued to hiss and growl.

"Help her, Ron," Clay's voice quivered.

"Maureen," I called to her again and again.

She raised her head. Her eyes were no longer her own—her usually green eyes now dark and piercing. A sight I had seen so many times before.

Lips peeled back, white teeth clenched tightly, she looked like a feral animal ready to attack.

Whatever was occupying Maureen's body had to go.

"I don't care who you are. It's time to leave."

Maureen growled, louder this time.

"Shut up."

Ignoring my words, Maureen sprung to her feet and lunged at me.

The battle had begun.

I raised my arms and met her advance. "Leave her. It's not your body."

She staggered backward, planting her feet, lunging once again.

This time I was ready and grabbed hold of her upper arms. Deflecting her blows, I spun her around, exposing her back. I threw her into a full nelson as we fell to the ground. Arms locked, we rolled over dirt and twigs. I tightened my grip as pain seethed from the healing wound of my open-heart surgery.

As we gasped for breath, I heard the collective voice of the group. "Maureen, fight! Come back to us."

Stacy stepped closer, extending her hand. She uttered, "May white light protect you."

"In the name of our Lord, leave her," Clay added, to no avail.

Maureen continued to snarl like a trapped animal.

Exhaustion setting in, I made one last-ditch effort. Catching my breath, I yelled, "Maureen, push him out! Come back. Push him out."

She continued to struggle. Just then, an ear-piercing scream ripped the air. She sounded more animal than human. A wounded animal. This was my moment. I could feel her resistance waning. I called out to Clay, "Get the holy water.

"Push him out. Push him out."

Then just as quickly as it started, the struggle ended.

Maureen's breathing, previously raspy, began to slow. "Are you okay, Kid?" I said, sensing she had reclaimed her body.

Gasping for breath, she nodded yes.

Maureen lifted herself off me and then collapsed once again, her back pinning me against the cold uneven earth. "I can't move," she said, her breathing labored.

Unable to move right away, we lay there. "Give me the holy water," I shouted over Maureen's drained body.

Special blend now in hand, I began to spray. The delicate odor of liquid sage permeated the air, as the fine droplets found their mark. "You okay, Kid?" I said, patting her shoulder. In an attempt to lighten the moment, I added, "It makes a great bug spray too, you know."

Silence. My attempt at banter fell on deaf ears.

Above our labored breath, Clay's voice echoed in the night. "Way to fight, Maureen. That was a nasty thing. We saw it on Dan's camera materializing in the woods just before it took you over."

What seemed like an eternity we lay on the ground. Gaining our strength, we slowly stood, climbed down off the bank, and began dusting ourselves off. Like a baboon grooming its mate, Stacy reached over and plucked sticks and twigs from our clothes. *It's so nice to be loved.*

The sound of distant footsteps drew my attention. I looked up to see the outline of Ron Jr.'s form cresting the hill. He shouted from where he stood. "Dad, this way."

Despite what had just transpired, I knew we still had a job to do, and the night was still young. Looking at each member of the team, finally coming to rest on Maureen, I asked, "Are we ready?"

With no objections, I started walking in Ron Jr.'s direction, the rest of the group close to my heels. Although they kept up, I sensed they were ready to call it a night.

Shortly after, we reached a clearing at the edge of a small lake. Beyond the lake, a rocky ledge rose out high into the night sky. As we stood there, the quiet was displaced by bouts of laughter, echoing from a bonfire above us, high atop the ledge. We were soon joined by Andrew and Chris. Surveying our surroundings, flashlight in hand, I stepped on a flat rock at the water's edge. As I scanned the horizon, I couldn't help but hear my son from the background. "That's a recipe for failure." His words drew laughter from the team.

Clay's voice called out, "Shoot at the cliffs, Dan."

Dan raised his camera to the tree line, scanning the top of the ledge.

Clay peered over his shoulder. "Wow, doesn't that look like Native Americans on horseback?" He hesitated. "That's absolutely wild. They look like they're watching us."

"Maybe it's just my mind playing tricks on me, but you see here," Dan said, pointing to the screen on the thermal imager. "Right here, it looks like galloping horses."

Off to my left, I caught movement in my peripheral vision. I turned to find Maureen with her makeshift pendulum in hand and arm extended, pointing over the still water. "Ron, I think there's a time slip there."

"Maureen, are you picking up on any Indians on horseback? 'Cause Dan and I have been seeing what appears to be Indians on horseback, up there, just watching us," Clay said.

Maureen turned her attention back to dowsing, "Are there any Soul Seekers here?"

As the silver bauble danced in the night, a splash cut through the stillness of the water. "Did you hear that?"

"Yes, I did." A shiver of apprehension crept up my spine. "What are Soul Seekers?"

"Ron, I asked if there were Soul Seekers here, and now it's pointing in the direction of the water."

"They're getting closer. I hear them," Clay piped up.

"I think it's probably time we should leave," I said, addressing the group.

Maureen interrupted. "We're being watched by the way, too."

"Watched, like last time watched?" Clay asked, then turned toward Dan. "Dan, can you scan the lake again?" As if realizing that Dan hadn't heard him, he repeated himself. "Do a scan of the lake, a complete scan. Maureen says we're being watched, like we were last time."

I took a step toward Dan and Clay. "Put your cameras down for a minute. Tell me if it's just me. I'm getting a feeling. Something's not right—"

Just then, Ron Jr.'s voice drew my attention. "Maureen! Maureen," he called.

My instincts kicked in. The feeling of dread overtook me.

I turned. Before me was Maureen. With her hand to her head, she stared at the ground. Ron Jr.'s hand was on her shoulder in an attempt to steady her. I surveyed the all-too-familiar scene unfolding before me. "Let her be," I said.

A growl escaped Maureen's lips as she attempted to pull away. To Ron Jr., still clinging to Maureen, I said, "Let her go. Give her room."

"Okay," Ron Jr. said as he took a step back.

"Ron, let me know if you want me to take her down," Chris said, sounding all too eager.

"Maureen, you got to push him out. You got to push him out, Kid." Oblivious to my words, she continued to back away. "Maureen! Maureen!"

"Watch her. She's going back too far," Clay spoke up.

"Don't let her get near the water," Stacy added, her voice quivering, as Maureen continued to retreat toward the water's edge.

With hands on thighs, Maureen contorted her face as she released a sinister laugh.

I strode toward her. As I drew closer, she took another step back, yanked the camera strap from her shoulder, tossing her costly Canon to the hard ground.

"Ah, crap."

Now, dangerously close, I had to act. Still too far away.

I raced forward.

I lunged at her, pulling her arms in a full nelson, as we dropped to the ground.

Without hesitation, like a linebacker completing a play, Chris dove at her legs, pinning them to the ground, while she continued to thrash about.

With urgency, Clay's voice echoed in the background. "Get the holy water."

Through clenched teeth, the creature within her struggling body released an ear-piercing shriek. Face down in the loose gravel, with the strength of ten men, she yanked her arms free from my grasp and wailed again.

As she bucked and clawed at the ground, I slipped my arm beneath hers and bore down on her, tightening my grip. "Leave this body. It's not your own. We command it. In the name of the Father, Son, and Holy Spirit." I felt its force against my chest, as the entity bucked and writhed beneath me. "Leave her. I command you."

Moaning, Maureen collapsed beneath my grasp. The moment I heard the shallow intake of her breath, I knew we had claimed victory.

"Son of a bitch," said Ron.

Ron's words, which had been distant, far away, suddenly became clearer.

Slowly, feeling as if I were fighting through gauze, I struggled to regain my senses. Face planted in the dirt, against the weight of Ron pressed against my back, I labored to rise. With the flat of my hand digging into the gravel, I stiffened my arms and raised myself onto my elbows.

I heard Clay's voice as he drew closer. "Are you all right, Maureen?"

My throat dry, my tongue gritty, I heaved a sigh. "Shit."

"Shit is right. I'm getting too old for this," Ron said as he leaned back and gave me some breathing room. "Chris, get off her."

No longer pinned to the ground, I slowly sat up. I inhaled sharply and coughed, forcibly ejecting debris from my mouth. Beneath the coating of dust, the bitter taste of blood, like I'd just eaten a mouthful of pennies, nearly gagged me. "Disgusting." I wiped my mouth. Nothing. It was dry.

I stood, brushed the dust off my pants and coat.

"Are you all right?" Ron asked.

"I still feel weird." I hesitated, not knowing how to put my thoughts into words.

"Weird?" Ron stood beside me. "What do you mean weird?"

"Through it all, your voice was far away. And I had the odd sensation, like I almost had claws. I was climbing trees, stalking prey." I paused and raised my hand to my mouth. "I swear. It tastes like blood. Honest to God, it tastes like blood."

"Are you sure you didn't bite your tongue?"

"Yeah, I'm sure. And you know what? Whatever it is, is still here."

With the last of my words, Ron spoke up, "Who's got a car? We got to get Maureen outta here."

Chris took a step toward us. "I do. It's over there."

"Okay, let's go."

With each step down the path toward the car, I felt the pull of the beast getting stronger, as if not willing to let me slip though his grasp so easily.

"Chris, are we getting closer. I think we need to leave. Now!"

Just as I spoke, we crested the hill, and the Jeep came into view. None too soon.

Moments later, we were on our way. With Chris driving and Andrew in the back, I suddenly felt uncomfortable. With Ron and the team making their way back to the parking lot by foot, I suddenly felt very alone. As the headlights cut a path through the darkness in front of us, the awkward silence was only broken by the sound of rocks being kicked up by the tires.

As the parking lot came into view, I suddenly realized that the tingling of energy that had terrorized me mere minutes ago was gone. Now, I couldn't help but pray that Ron and group would hurry up and get here. The wall of silence was thickening, and it was all I could do but wonder what Andrew and Chris were thinking. Two guys I barely knew. I sat twiddling my thumbs as they barely spoke a word to me.

Ron, where the hell are you?

Out of the corner of my eye, I caught the first beams from the team's flashlight and heaved a sigh of relief. "They're back."

Since we had completed the mission to provide Chris Balzano the material he needed to write his book, we packed the gear in Ron's car and said our good-byes. I couldn't help but be glad that this night was over. It certainly wasn't the walk in the woods I had thought it would be.

OUR THOUGHTS

MAUREEN:

I'm not sure what I expected when Ron told me we were going for a ride and ultimately going for a hike in the woods, but encountering a legendary creature was not one of them. Do I believe that I ended up channeling a Puckwudgie? To be honest, I don't know. In my experience, I have nothing that I could compare it to. What I can say is that my recollection was that whatever I was picking up on, or channeling, gave me the overwhelming sensation that I was running, jumping from tree to tree. Weird, I know. Oh yeah, after our little episode near the edge of the water, I had the unmistakable taste of copper in my mouth. Or should I say blood? So much so that when I ran my finger in my mouth, I absolutely expected to find the source. After all, after being tackled to the ground by Ron and Chris, sacked if you will, I wouldn't have been surprised to find out that I'd bitten my tongue. Oddly enough. My finger was clean. There was NO blood. At least, not in this realm.

RON:

What started out to be a lighthearted investigation, a means to test our portable equipment in an outside environment, turned ominous when we encountered an unknown, mythical creature. As we were led deeper into the woods, we were dogged by a dark shadow that finally showed itself in the thermal imager, seconds before the first attack ensued.

The second encounter took a more frightening turn when I dislocated my finger. Maureen, through her channeling, unwillingly relived the horror of the creature as her own. Was this the mythical Puckwudgie? By viewing the following, you can decide for yourself.

Maureen's trance channeling of her encounter with the Puckwudgie at Freetown State Forest can be seen through the CD of Chris Balzano's book, *Picture Yourself Ghost Hunting*, or on YouTube at *https://www.youtube. com/watch?v=g4kKSQAmjbY*. It can also be viewed in the documentary titled *The Bridgewater Triangle* and on the television show *Monsters and Mysteries in America* on Destination America.

About the Authors

MAUREEN WOOD is a fifth-generation psychic/trance medium and is currently the lead psychic/medium for the New England Ghost Project and cohost of the popular *Ghost Chronicles* radio show.

RON KOLEK is the Emmy-winning founder and lead investigator of the New England Ghost Project. Ron produces and hosts *Ghost Chronicles* on Ghostvillage Radio, iTunes, and Podcast Alley.

Visit them at *ghostchroniclesthebook.com*.

To Our Readers

Weiser Books, an imprint of Red Wheel/Weiser, publishes books across the entire spectrum of occult, esoteric, speculative, and New Age subjects. Our mission is to publish quality books that will make a difference in people's lives without advocating any one particular path or field of study. We value the integrity, originality, and depth of knowledge of our authors.

Our readers are our most important resource, and we appreciate your input, suggestions, and ideas about what you would like to see published.

Visit our website at *www.redwheelweiser.com* to learn about our upcoming books and free downloads, and be sure to go to *www.redwheelweiser.com/newsletter* to sign up for newsletters and exclusive offers.

You can also contact us at *info@rwwbooks.com* or at

Red Wheel/Weiser, LLC
65 Parker Street, Suite 7
Newburyport, MA 01950